HAL•LEONARD

BANJO PLAY-ALONG

Pete Seeger

Cover Photo © Andy Freeberg / Retna Ltd.

Clawhammer Banjo Arrangements by Michael J. Miles
www.MilesMusic.org

Up-Picking Banjo Arrangements by Mike Kropp

Recording credits:
Vocals – Michael J. Miles, Elaine Moore, Bill Brickey
Clawhammer Banjo, Guitar – Michael J. Miles
Up-Picking Banjo – Mike Kropp
Double Bass, Recording Engineer – John Abbey

ISBN 978-1-4803-9494-0

Melody Trails, Inc.

 The Richmond Organization

EXCLUSIVELY DISTRIBUTED BY

HAL•LEONARD®
CORPORATION
7777 W. BLUEMOUND RD. P.O. BOX 13819 MILWAUKEE, WI 53213

Visit Hal Leonard Online at
www.halleonard.com

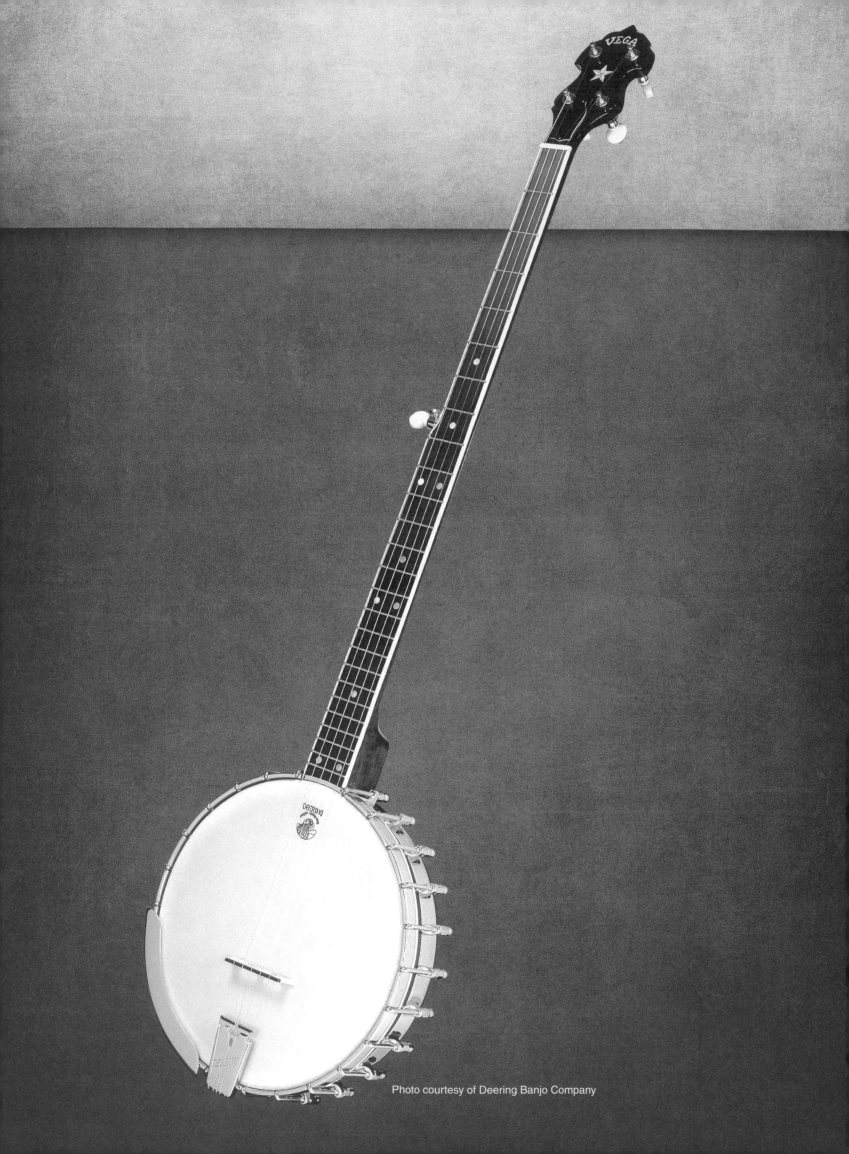

Photo courtesy of Deering Banjo Company

Pete Seeger

FORCES IT TO SURRENDER

THIS MACHINE SURROUNDS HATE

DEERING
banjo company
STRINGED INSTRUMENTS

Photo courtesy of Deering Banjo Company

Performance Notes
By Michael Miles and Mike Kropp

Pete was everybody's banjo player with musical influences that stretched across the entire world, as well as a warm and caring heart that went even further. Nobody plays these songs exactly like Pete. He was ever playful with them and always watchful of the people around him, ready to respond to the room and turn on a dime, from a whisper to a whistle, from a yodel to a shout. We both had the privilege of singing with, playing with, and knowing Pete Seeger. And yes, we are so very fortunate to be able to say that. He touched both of our lives for decades and it is with the greatest respect and honor that we share these songs with you.

Included here are eight classic songs from Pete's world. He did not play banjo on all of them as he often used his guitar for song accompaniment. But in this collection, for banjo players, we have created banjo parts in both up-picking and clawhammer technique. Pete was skilled at both of these right-hand banjo styles and moved freely between them. You can play along in the style that you prefer, or play them both (one at a time). There are also banjo harmony lines for some of the songs.

The parts are identified on the first page of each song, and then the tablature is written like a musical score with one part on top of the other. For example, look at "Blue Skies" on page 12 and notice that the top line says "Banjo 1 (up-picking)" and the lower line says "Banjo 2 (clawhammer)." Pick whichever part you'd prefer to play, and then play away. Be sure to stay on the right line!

We feature three-part vocal harmonies in this collection of songs. These vocal parts are included in the spirit of the Weavers, the Almanac Singers, and the singing union hall meeting. Our intention is to make the experience of playing the banjo parts more enjoyable, and more in the actual context of the songs.

Please pay attention to the banjo tuning and the use of capos. Several different tunings are used across this collection, and often when there is an up-picking and clawhammer part played simultaneously, the banjos are in the same key but using different tunings. And when a capo is used, remember that the 5th string must also be raised the same number of frets to sound correct. Look in the upper left hand corner on the first page of each song to see how the banjos are tuned, and if a capo is used. The Roman numeral indicates on which fret the capo is to be placed.

TRY THE BASIC STRUM
Here is Pete's "Basic Strum," as he portrayed it in his book on how to play the banjo. This strum provides a basic folk song accompaniment that any banjo player can use to accompany just about any song. Before we step into the actual songs, feel the heart of Pete Seeger's rhythm by strumming a few chords on the banjo.

The Basic Strum

C tuning:
(5th-1st) G-C-G-B-D

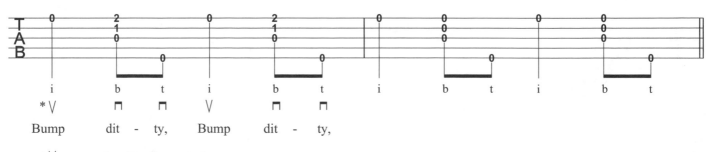

* V = upstroke, ⊓ = downstroke

This is known as *bump ditty*. Note that the first note, "bump" is done with the index finger picking upward. The next notes –"ditty"–are a brush down with the middle finger followed by the thumb playing the 5th string.

Our recommendation is to play the basic strum over and over again until you get a good groove going with it. Watch a movie and do the basic strum as a sound track. By the time the movie is over, you should have the feel of it and be ready to play any song. Pete's friend Woody said, "If you know two chords, you can play all the good songs. If you know three chords you can play the fancy songs, too." And if you can do the basic strum on the banjo, you change the world. That's what Pete did. Enjoy.

"We Shall Overcome"

The top line of the tablature sketches the melody to the song. The lower line is a harmony. On the recording, both of these are played clawhammer style, but the harmony line could easily be adapted for up-picking as well. A third choice is simply to play the chords and make up your own part.

There are, in all of these songs, choices and adjustments for you to make. Left-hand fingering is always an issue, as is note location. In G tuning, any open string can be played as a fretted note and many fretted notes can easily be played on an adjacent string at a different location. We give recommendations, but in the folk process there's no exact right way.

"Blue Skies"

This is truly a banjo duet, where the melody and harmony parts are traded back and forth between Banjo 1 (up-picking) and Banjo 2 (clawhammer). Here's how that works. The song form is Verse, Verse, Bridge, Verse. Also known as A-A-B-A.

As the recording begins, Banjo 1 plays the melody for the A section, while Banjo 2 plays harmony. On page 13, line 2, the B section begins and Banjo 2 takes the melody, and Banjo 1 goes to harmony. On page 13, line 4, they switch back.

Notice the opening four chords: Em–Em/D♯–Em/D–Em/C♯. The letter after the slash indicates the bass note. For example, Em/D♯ means an Em chord with a D♯ in the bass. You can hear that descending bass line in the guitar and bass accompaniment.

In our version, Banjo 1 also delivers that descending line in the upper register. Look at page 14, line 2, and notice that the first note of each measure plays those notes (E–D♯–D–C♯). It happens again in line 4 of the same page.

There are road signs (like **D.S. al Coda** and **D.C. al Coda**) in this collection that are important to know about. They are music engravers' attempts at saving trees and time by not having to write out the same thing over and over too many times.

D.S. al Coda means go back to the sign (𝄋) and play from there until it tells you to jump to the Coda. Play the Coda and you're done.

D.C. al Coda means go back to the very beginning, and play from there until it tells you to jump to the Coda. Play the Coda and you're done.

D.S.S. al Coda means go back to the double sign (𝄋 𝄋) and play from there until it tells you to jump to the Coda. Play the Coda and you're done.

"Get Up and Go"

On the one hand, this is a simple folk song. A young Pete Seeger played this song in the '60s on the Smothers Brothers' TV show, while sitting in a rocking chair, and just singing to the skies. He makes it look easy as he gives it his Pete Seeger warmth.

Pete named his simple banjo accompaniment "bump ditty." That corresponds to a quarter note followed by two eighth notes (see Figure 1). This song is in 3/4 time, so the mnemonic device would be "bump ditty ditty" (see Figure 2). Sometimes for variation and because of tempo, that gets played as "bump bump ditty." This is also known as Pete's *waltz strum.*

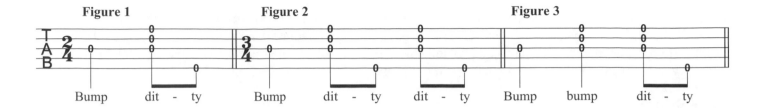

If you plan to up-pick this song, before reading the tablature, just try this chord progression using a simple "bump ditty ditty" accompaniment.

Get your right hand going smoothly. Up-pick that first beat, and follow it with two brush thumbs. That is the underlying "groove" throughout this song. Given your control of that from the up-picking perspective, then you can step into the tablature and see all the variations that are possible.

There are a few things that are important to notice about this song:
1. The two banjos are in different tunings.
2. The click at the start of the recording demonstrates why it says at the opening of the song that it is "very fast, in one." You'll hear 4 clicks, but each click represents a full measure.
3. The figure (♩♩ = ♩♪) indicates that the song is played with swing feel.
4. Rhythm Figures: Banjo 2 has three 16-measure Rhythm Figures. These are variations played clawhammer style that accompany Banjo 1. On pages 23 and 24, you'll notice that those Rhythm Figures are recalled, indicating that they are to be played again, but to save space they are not written out again.
5. Fill Box: At the bottom of page 21 is Fill 1, in a box. It replaces Line 3, Measure 3 on the subsequent verses.

Up-pickers, be sure to check out the solos on page 23 and 24. They take the simple folk song and demonstrate some of the possible magic within.

"If I Had a Hammer"
This song is sacred ground in America, as it has touched the lives of so many people. It is the source for the name of *Sing Out* magazine. It is at the heart of American folk music. And aren't we the lucky ones who get to play it?

The pickup notes to the song start, not on the first beat of a measure, but on the "and" of beat 2. Look at page 29, second line, last measure, to see how the pickup measure looks in the middle of the song as a complete measure.

Look at the bottom of page 28 to see **Fill 1** and **Fill 2**. Now notice the recall labels just below the Verse section heading above the first measure on the page. These fills fit in as variations of the up-picking part on the repeats. They portray what is on the recording. The bottom line is the chord progression, and the variations on the recording demonstrate that sometimes you may hit two strings or three strings or one string, but if you're on the right chord with the forward moving right-hand groove, then all of those options will work and can be used for dynamic variation.

The clawhammer part is in a different tuning than the up-picking part. It opens with a rhythmic accompaniment, and then on page 28 it picks up the melody. The sound of the two banjos together here is, in part, our tribute to Pete for bringing the banjo to so many of us. Please play this one with your banjo picking friends, just as we played it together.

"Kisses Sweeter than Wine"

This song was written by Huddie Ledbetter, aka Lead Belly, with words by the Weavers. Pete and Lead Belly were friends, and Pete described his tunes as "some of the best songs we'll ever know." In tribute to Lead Belly, Pete made an album of his songs and when he played this one, he usually used his 12-string guitar, in part because that was what Lead Belly played. But it also makes for a beautiful banjo song with the exotic pull between major and minor, as well as the interjection of periodic measures of 2/4 time. On page 31, line 2, last measure, notice that the time signature is 2/4 for one measure only, and then back to 4/4 on line 3. The chorus ends on an E major chord, which gives it a surprising lift away from the E minor sound in the key of G.

There are a few things to watch closely for. Look at page 31, line 4, measure 3. This is where the E chord arrives with a full chord hammer-on. The full chord hammer-on adds drama and buys you an extra moment to get your fingers in place. Be careful whenever the E chord comes up that you do not play the open 5th string, as that is not in the chord and will sour the sound of the E major chord.

Now look at page 31, line 5, measures 2 and 3. Both of these measures include open string pull-offs. In the music, there is a half slur attached to the open 1st string. Use any available left-hand finger to pull that note off and sound the open string.

"Wimoweh"

For this song, Pete would strum a few chords and teach the whole world to sing in harmony. If you ever were in a room where it happened, or even saw a film clip of this song, you felt the electrifying power of the sound of the banjo. This is the classic example of Pete using the banjo as an amazing tool to drive the song forward. While we have a lot of detail to share about ways to approach it, along with melody and harmony, we strongly recommend that you approach this song first without tab as Pete did—with the chord progression firmly in place, use a whamming approach to playing the banjo.

Here's the chord progression that repeats over and over throughout the entire song.

| C | F | C | G ||

Here's what whamming looks like:

Whamming

C tuning:
(5th-1st) G-C-G-B-D

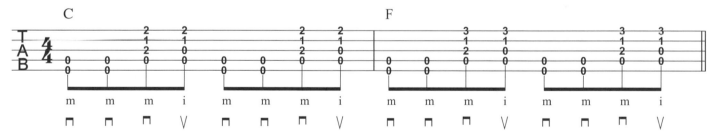

Whamming works with three down-strums with the middle finger, and one up-strum with the index finger. Pete liked it because he could do it loudly and help the room stay together. On the recording, the whamming starts when the vocal starts. Listen to how it makes the rhythm start to swing and drive forward. That is the heart of the matter right there. In the tablature, Banjo 1 is doing the *whamming*.

There are three clawhammer banjo parts from which to choose. Banjo 2 plays a clawhammer rhythm that compliments the whamming. Banjo 3 plays the Wimoweh melody. Banjo 4 plays the harmony line.

"Turn! Turn! Turn!"

This one is clawhammer only, but with the chord progression outlined and the melody sketched in the tablature. You could also create an up-picking version. It is a magnificent song. There are a just a few rhythmic twists that need attention. At the end of the first line, there is a bracket over the last three notes, with a small "3" within the bracket. This is called a triplet, where the time reserved for two quarter notes (or four eighth notes) is equally divided into three. That is what gives the words, "To ev'ry" its distinctive character and emphasized rhythm.

You'll notice on the recording and see in the tablature that the triplet figure both recurs and at times is played differently. Such is the nature of live performance folk music. Pete's emphasis was always on the message. He was a fine player, but he would say that it's okay to play it this way one time and differently the next. We include this to emphasize the priorities that matter. Yes, it is a triplet, but as a player you can and will vary that—and what matters most is not the delivery of the triplet but the heart of the song.

"Sailing Down My Golden River"

There are three verses to this beautiful song. On Verses 1 and 3, the banjo plays the melody along with the vocals. Verse 2 has a simpler, rhythmic accompaniment. Listen for a simple bass note and strum. As with all of these songs, you are encouraged to mix and match the melody and the accompaniment as you prefer. The tempo clicks at the beginning of the recording give a half-note feel, which sets this up as a gentle ballad. That is why the tempo heading is noted as "Moderately in two."

CONCLUSION

Pete Seeger was our friend, our mentor, and a shining example of the citizen musician. Among his many vital actions was encouraging others to reach out, reach higher, and to sing out for what is right and for the joy of it. Folk songs are perfect for that. These are all folk songs that, when put in writing, can look quite complicated and intimidating. So play along with us, play along with Pete, and above all play along with the people in your world. There is no end to making music—there's always more to learn and always more to play.

PETE SEEGER
PO BOX 431
BEACON, NY 12508-0431

Thanks, Mike.
keep on
picking
Pete

Michael J. Miles

Wood engraving "Sloop Clearwater at Storm King" by Vic Schwarz • Cold Spring, NY 10516

We Shall Overcome

Musical and Lyrical Adaptation by Zilphia Horton, Frank Hamilton, Guy Carawan and Pete Seeger
Inspired by African American Gospel Singing, members of the Food and Tobacco Workers Union, Charleston, SC,
and the southern Civil Rights Movement

Key of C

G tuning, capo V:
(5th-1st) G-D-G-B-D

Intro/Banjo Solo
Moderately slow ♩ = 94

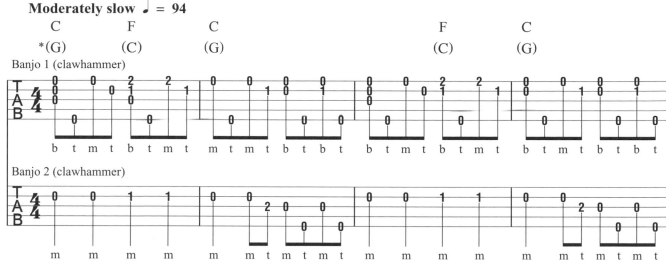

*Symbols in parentheses represent chord names respective to capoed banjos.
Symbols above reflect actual sounding chords. Capoed fret is "0" in tab.

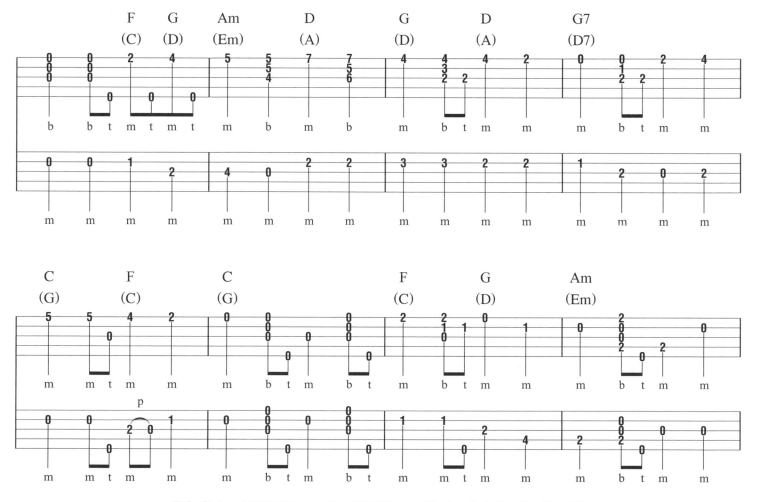

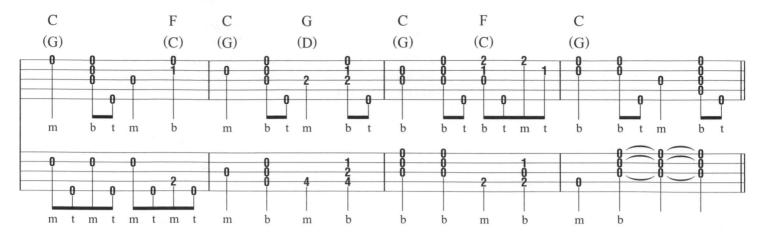

Verse

1. We shall o - ver - come. We shall o - ver - come.
2., 3. *See additional lyrics*

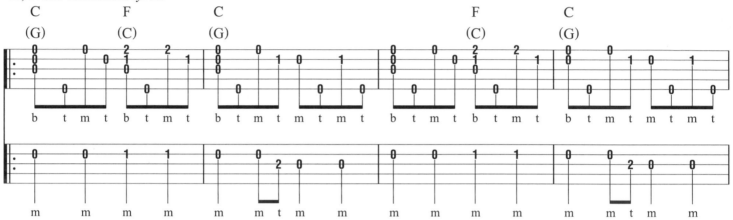

We shall o - ver - come some day - ay - ay.

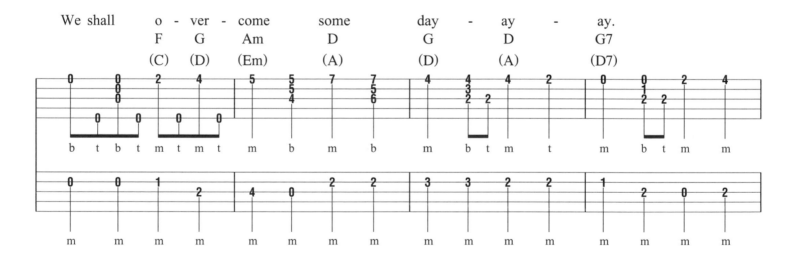

Deep in my heart I do be - lieve

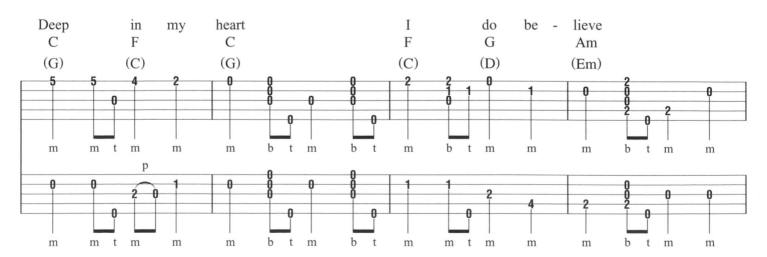

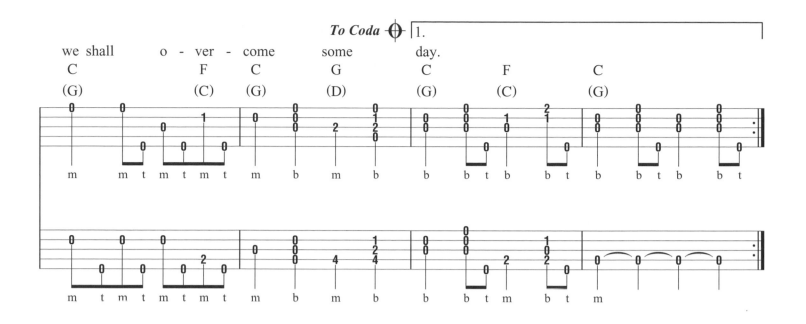

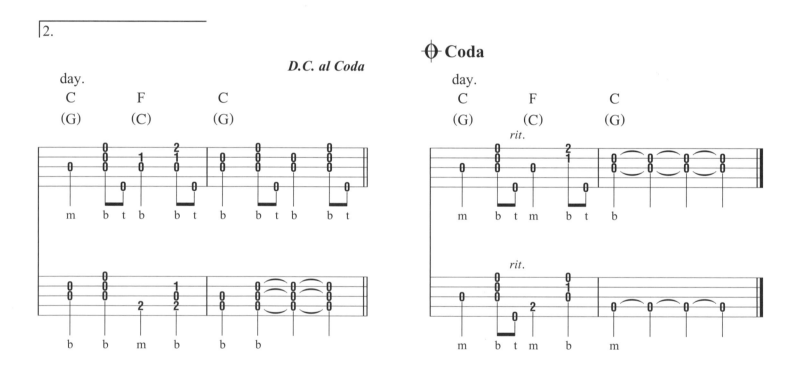

Additional Lyrics

2. We'll walk hand in hand.
   We'll walk hand in hand.
   We'll walk hand in hand some day.
   Deep in my heart I do believe
   We'll walk hand in hand some day.

3. The whole wide world around,
   The whole wide world around,
   The whole wide world around, some day.
   Deep in my heart I do believe
   We shall overcome some day.

Blue Skies

from BETSY

Words and Music by Irving Berlin

Key of G

G tuning:
(5th-1st) G-D-G-B-D

Intro

Moderately fast ♩ = 136

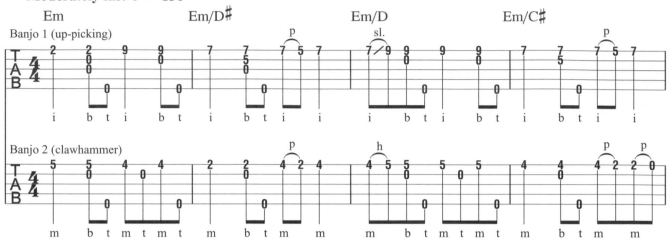

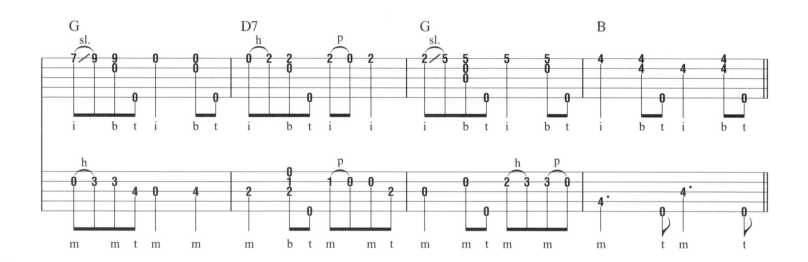

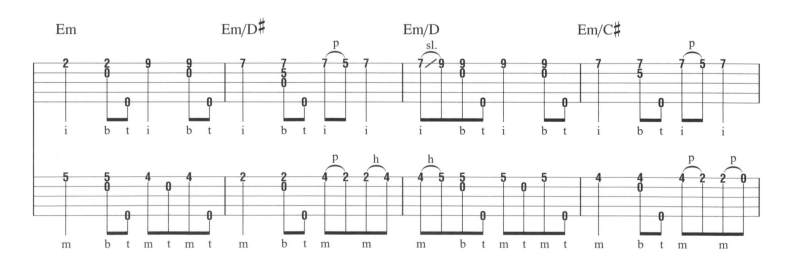

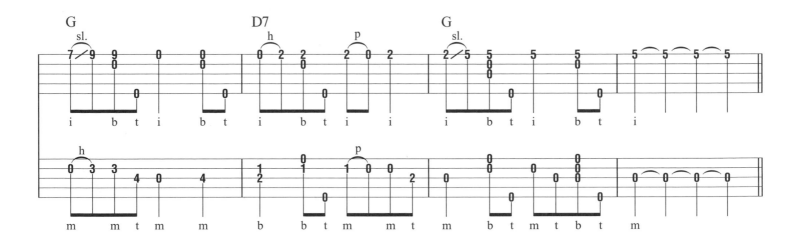

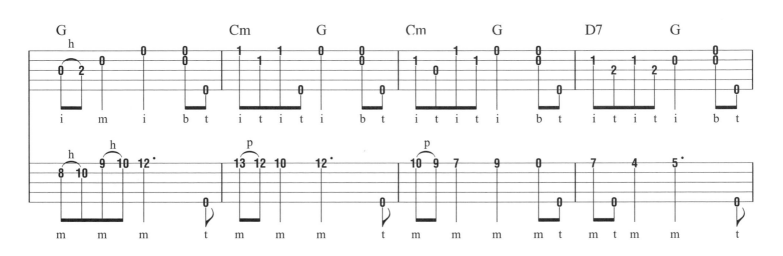

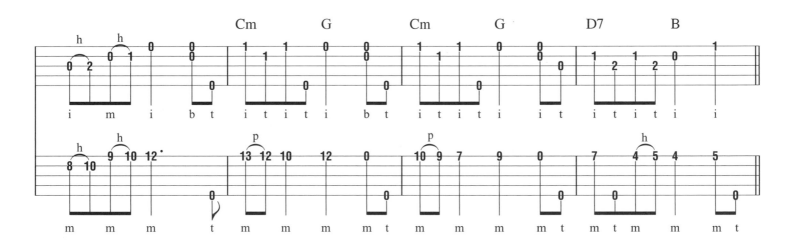

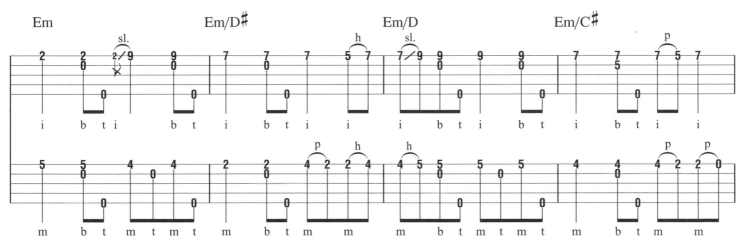

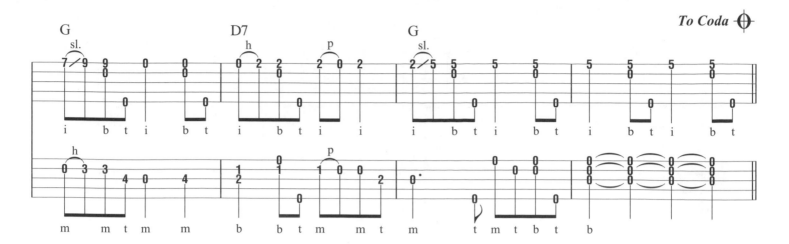

Verse

1. Blue   skies   smil-in' at   me,   noth-in' but

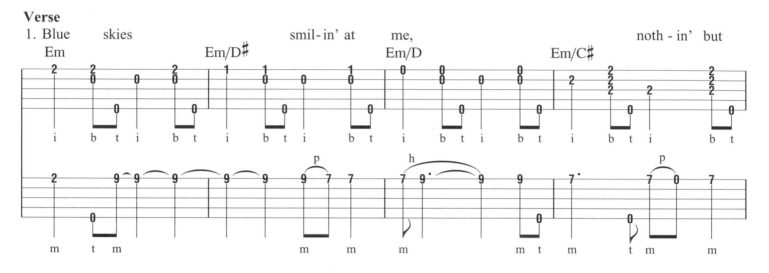

blue   skies   do I   see.

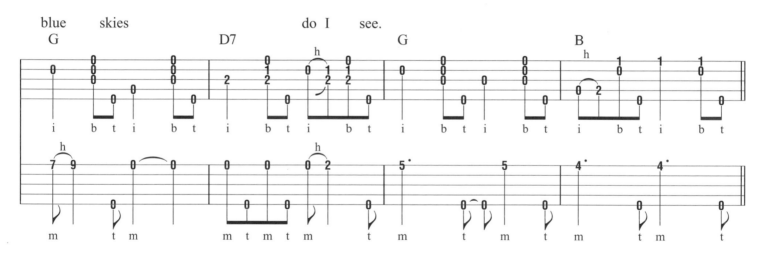

Verse

2. Blue   days,   all of them gone,   noth-in' but

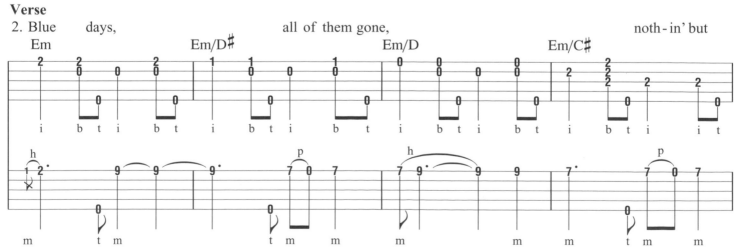

blue   skies   from now   on.

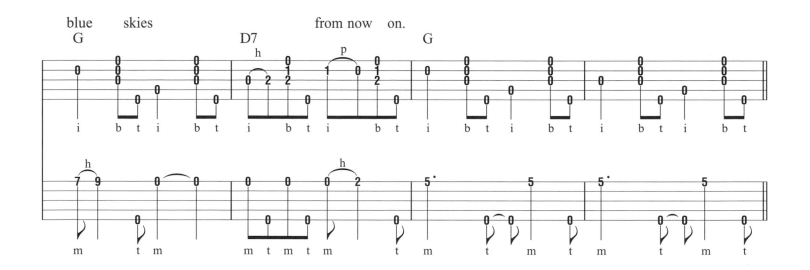

Bridge

Nev-er saw the sun   shin-in' so   bright.   Nev- er saw things   go-in' so   right.

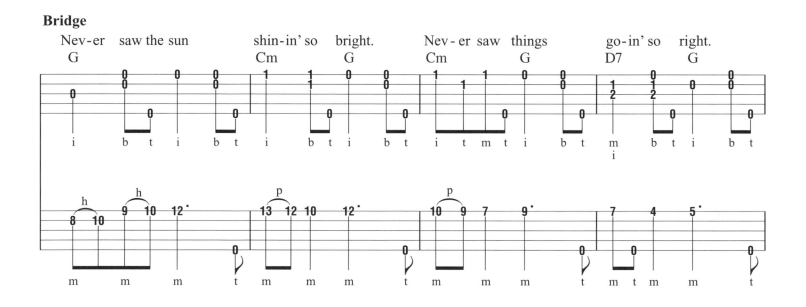

No-tic-ing the day   hur-ry-in' by,   when you're in love,   my how they fly.

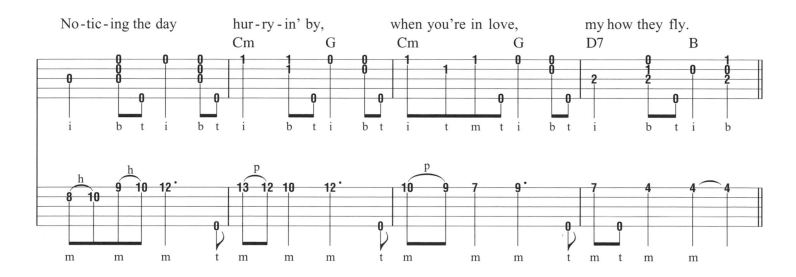

Verse

3. Blue   skies   smil-in' at me,   noth-in' but

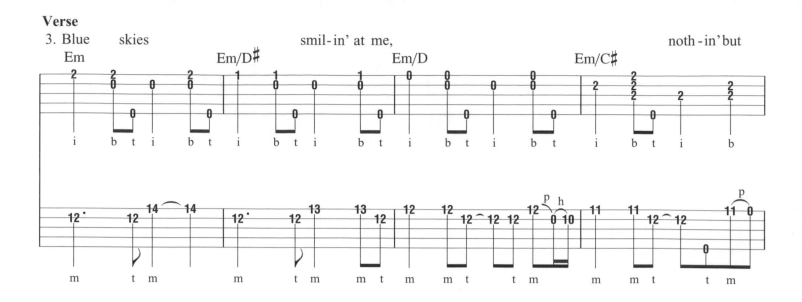

D.C. al Coda

blue   skies   do I   see.

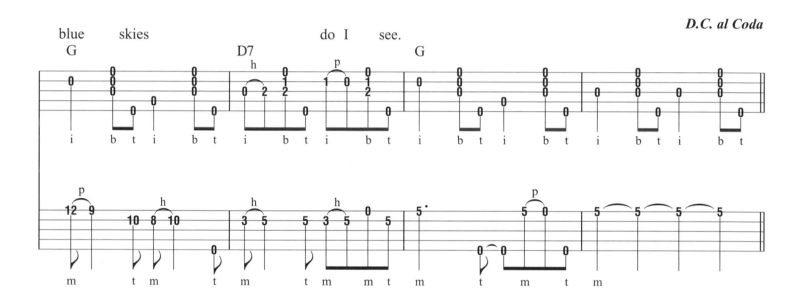

 Coda

Bridge

Nev-er saw the sun   shin-in' so bright.   Nev-er saw things   go-in' so right.

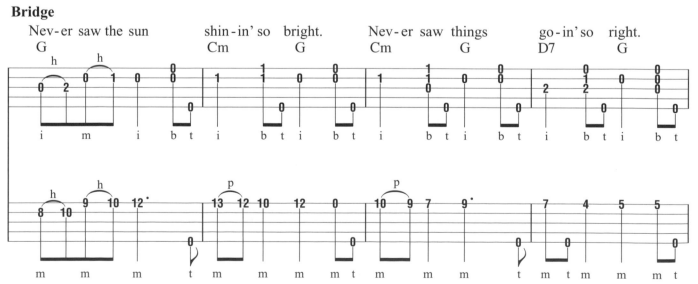

No-tic-ing the days   hur-ry-in' by,   when you're in love,   my how they fly.

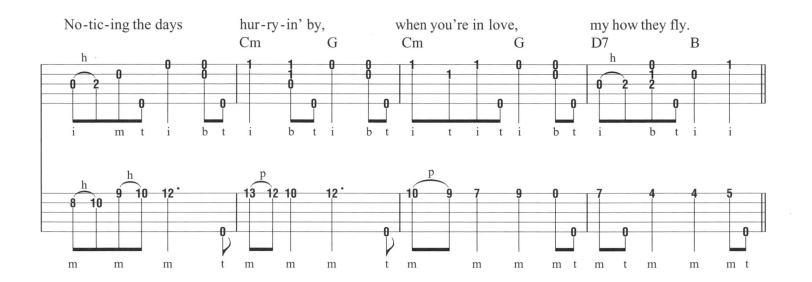

Verse

4. Blue   skies   smil-in' at me,   noth-in' but

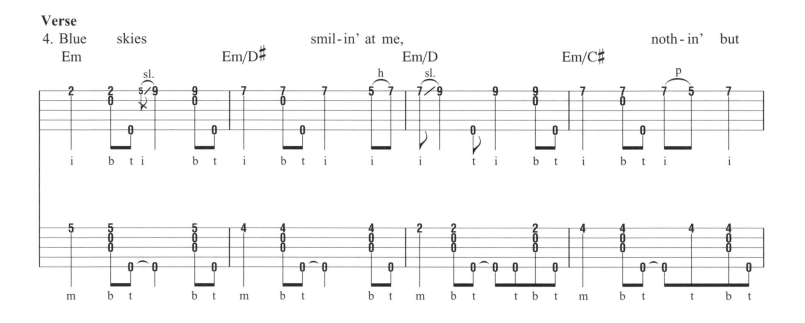

blue   skies   do I   see.

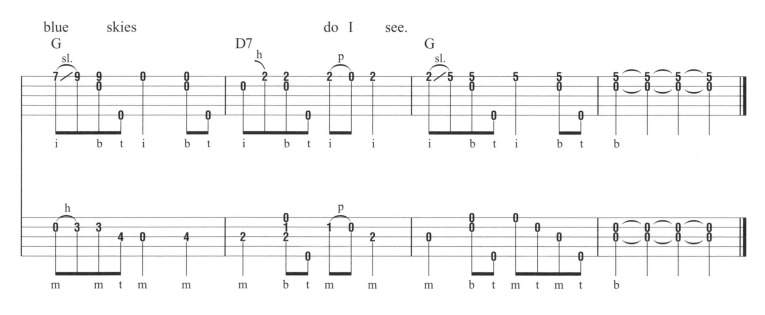

Get Up and Go

Words collected, adapted and set to Original Music by Pete Seeger

Key of C

Banjo 1: C tuning:
(5th-1st) G-C-G-B-D

Banjo 2: Double C tuning:
(5th-1st) G-C-G-C-D

Intro
Very fast, in One ♩ = **180**

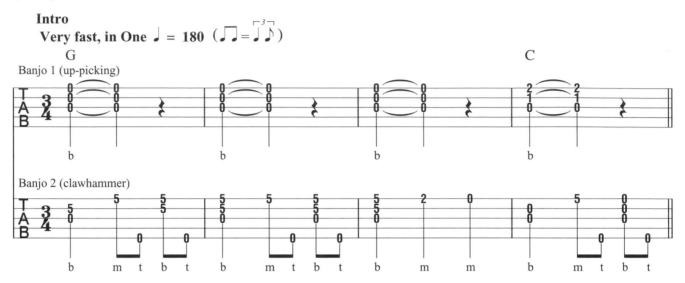

Chorus

How do I know my youth is all spent? My

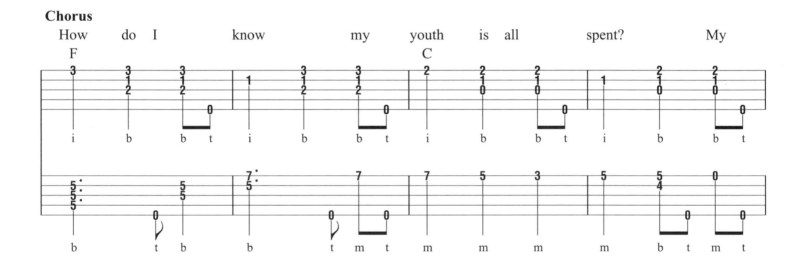

get up and go has got up and went. In

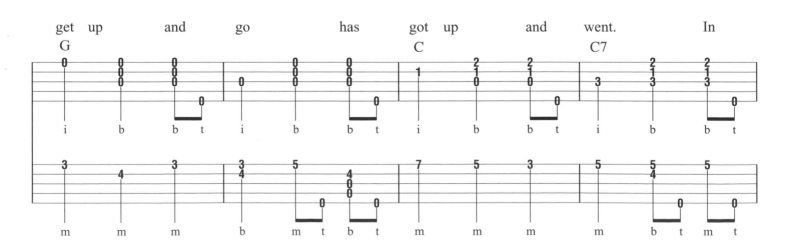

spite of it all, I'm a - ble to grin when I

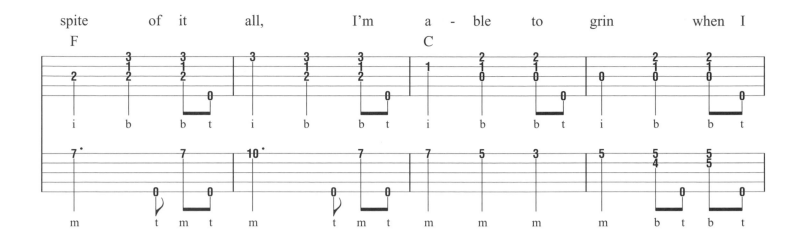

think of the plac - es my get up has been.

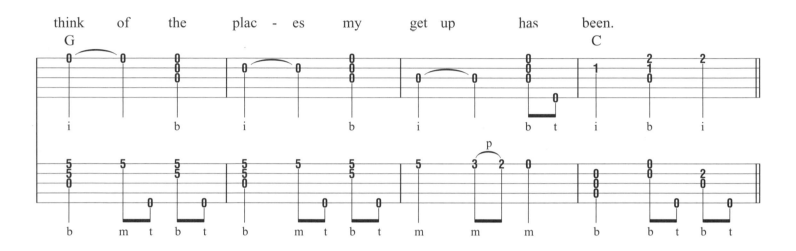

Interlude

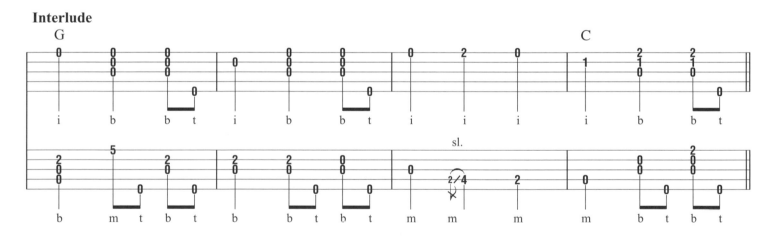

𝄋 **Verse**

1. Old age is gold - en, I think I've heard said, but
3. *See additional lyrics*

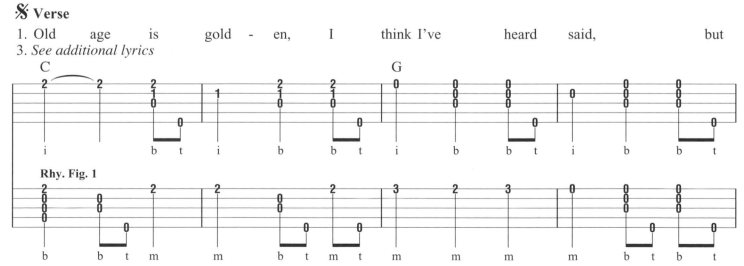

Rhy. Fig. 1

some - times   I   won - der   as I crawl   in - to   bed.   My

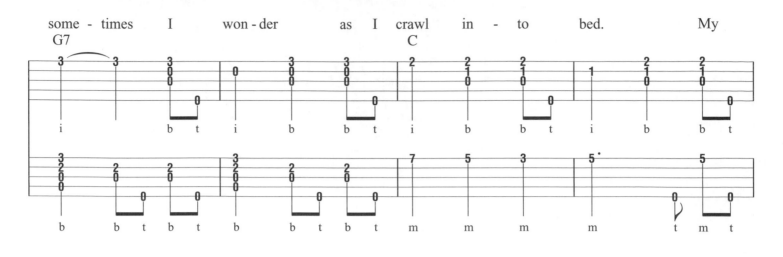

ears   in a drawer   my   teeth   in a   cup   my

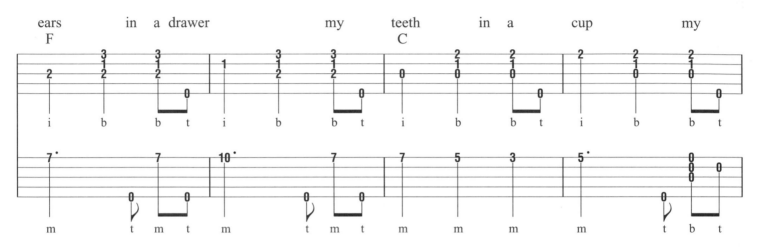

eyes   on   the   ta - ble   un - til I   wake   up.   2. As

End Rhy. Fig. 1

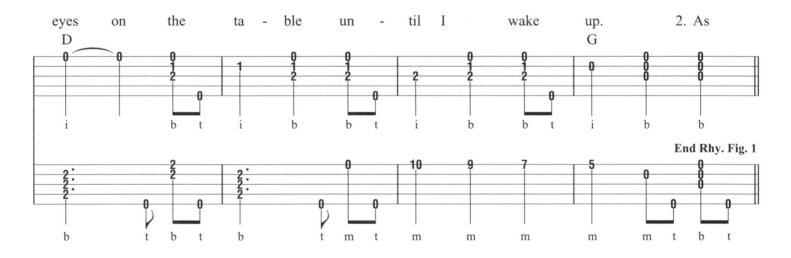

 Verse

sleep   dims   my   vi - sion   I   say   to my - self,   is there

4., 5. *See additional lyrics*

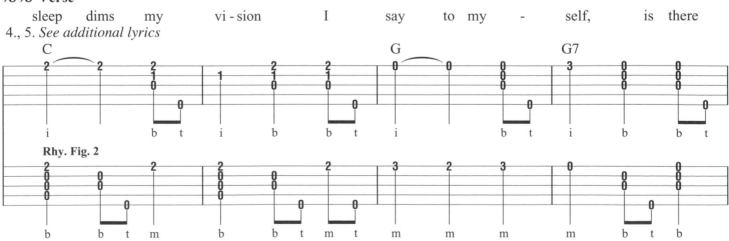

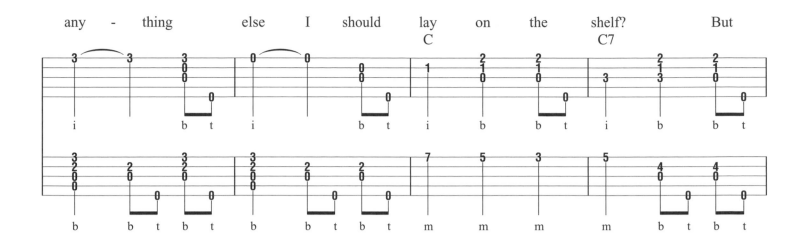

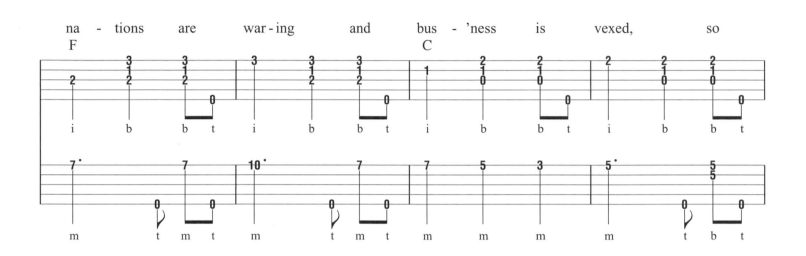

2nd & 3rd times, Banjo 2: w/ Fill 1

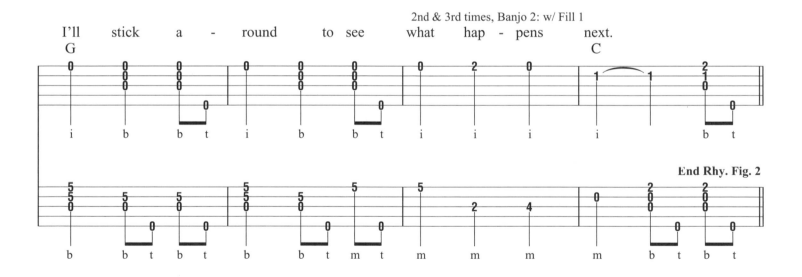

End Rhy. Fig. 2

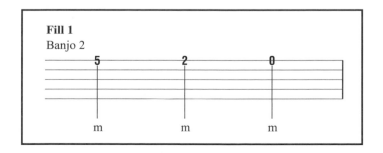

Chorus

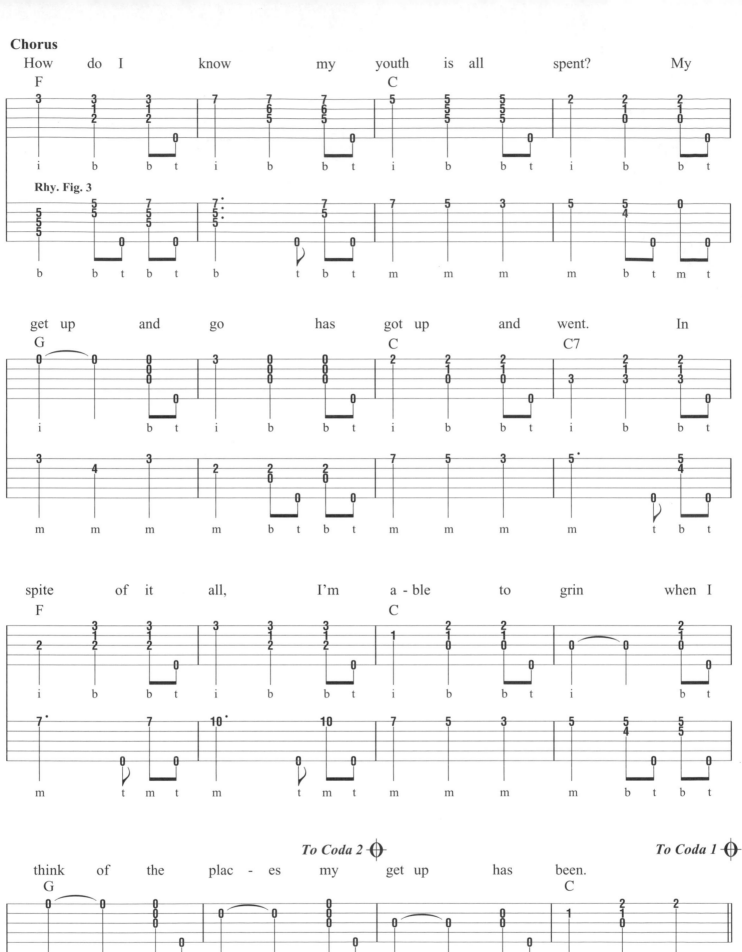

Interlude

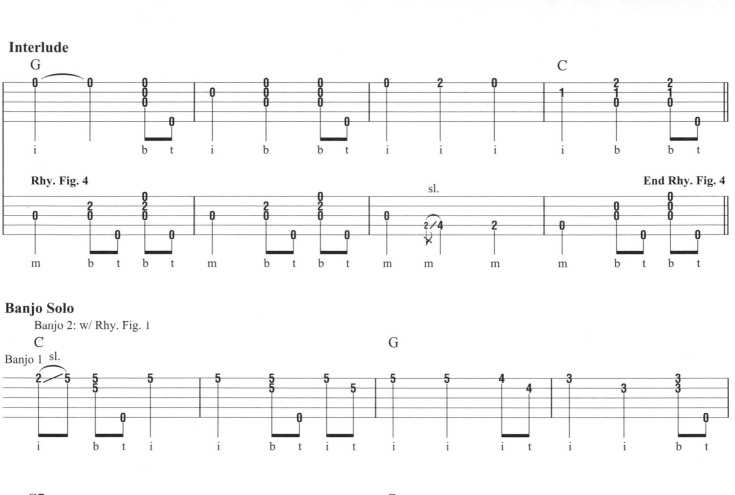

Rhy. Fig. 4

End Rhy. Fig. 4

Banjo Solo

Banjo 2: w/ Rhy. Fig. 1

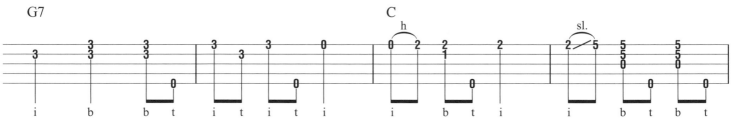

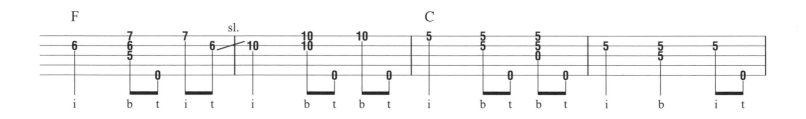

Banjo 2: w/ Rhy. Fig. 2

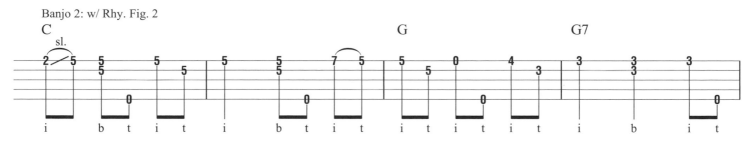

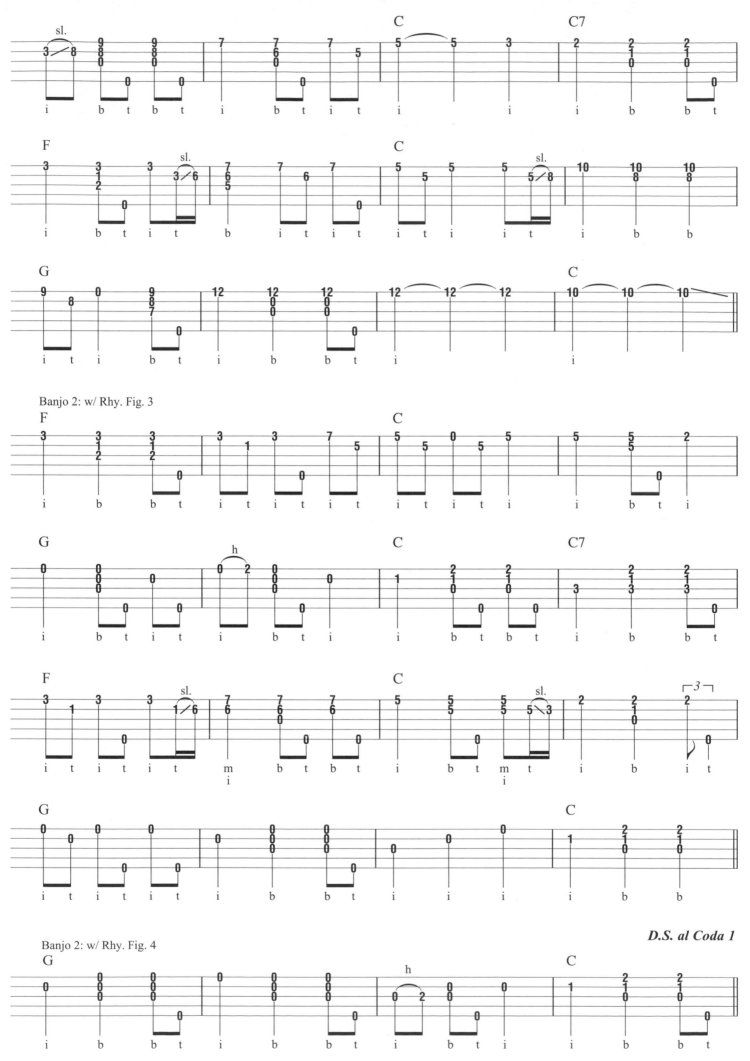

Banjo 2: w/ Rhy. Fig. 3

Banjo 2: w/ Rhy. Fig. 4

D.S. al Coda 1

24

⊕ Coda 1
Interlude

5. I get

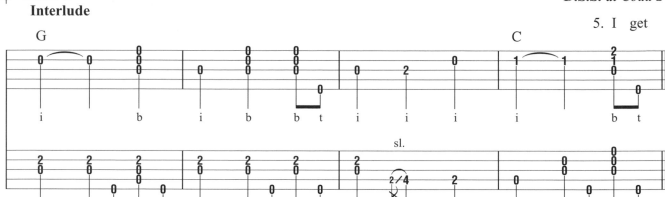

⊕ Coda 2

get   up   has   been.

Outro

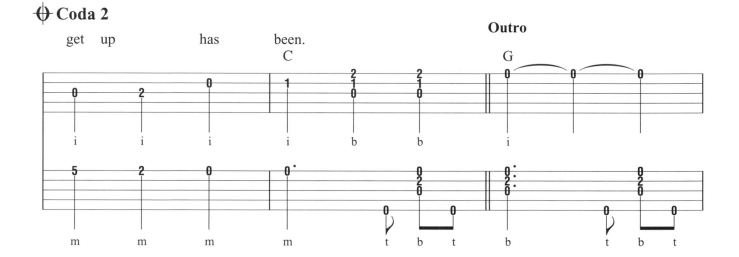

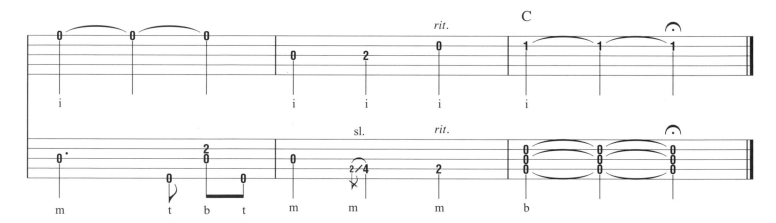

Additional Lyrics

3. When I was younger, my slippers were red.
   I could kick up my heels right over my head.
   When I was older, my slippers were blue
   But still I could dance the whole night through.

4. Now I am old, my slippers are black.
   I huff to the store and I puff my way back.
   But never you laugh, I don't mind at all,
   I'd rather be huffing than not puffing at all.

5. I get up each morning and dust off my wits,
   Open the paper and read the obits.
   If I'm not there, I know I'm not dead,
   So I eat a good breakfast and go back to bed.

If I Had a Hammer
(The Hammer Song)

Words and Music by Lee Hays and Pete Seeger

Key of C

Banjo 1: C tuning:
(5th-1st) G-C-G-B-D

Banjo 2: Double C tuning:
(5th-1st) G-C-G-C-D

𝄋 **Intro/Banjo Solo**

Fast ♩ = 152

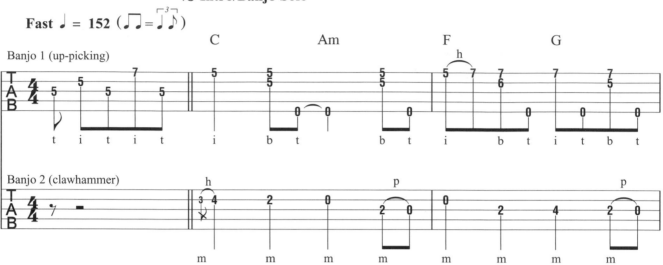

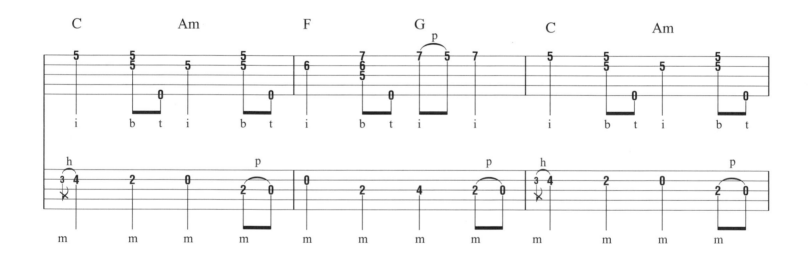

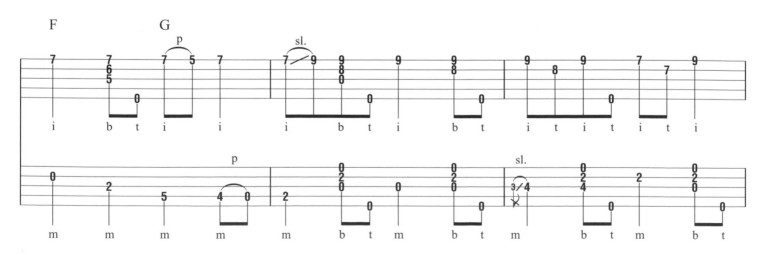

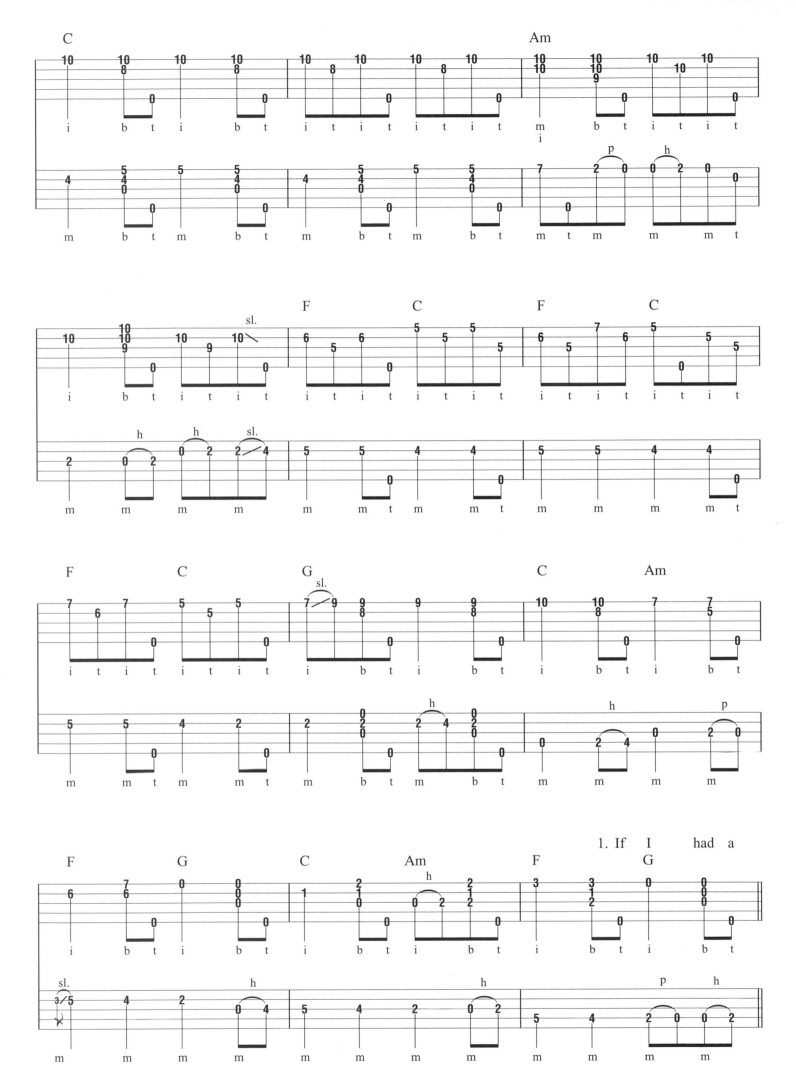

1. If   I   had a

Verse

2nd time, Banjo 1: w/ Fill 1 (2 times)
3rd time, Banjo 1: w/ Fill 2

ham - mer,   I'd   ham-mer in the morn   -   ing.   I'd   ham - mer in the

2., 3., 4. See additional lyrics

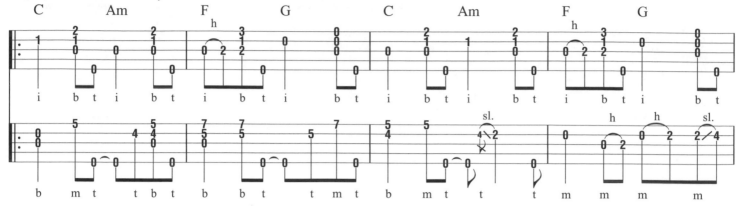

eve - ning,   all   o-ver this   land.   I'd   ham-mer out

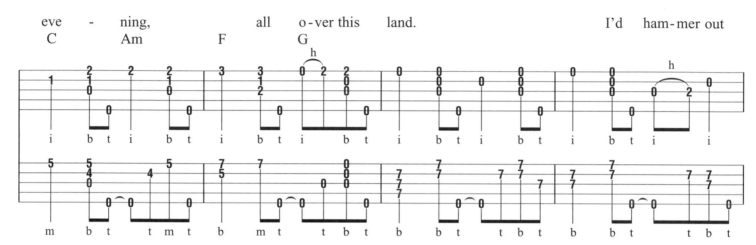

dan - ger.   I'd   ham-mer out   warn - ing.   I'd   ham-mer out

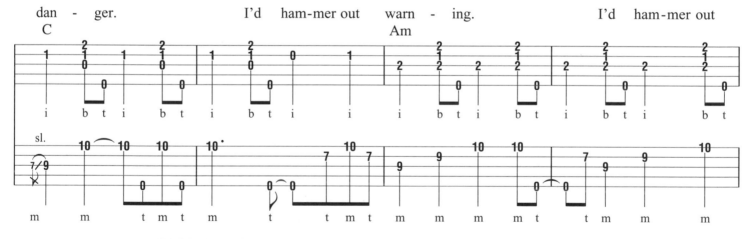

Fill 1
Banjo 1

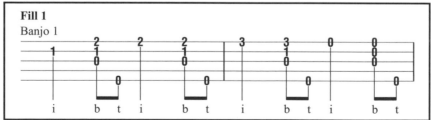

Fill 2
Banjo 1

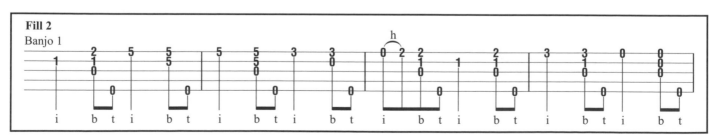

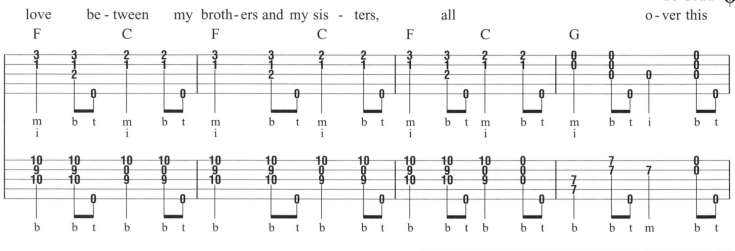

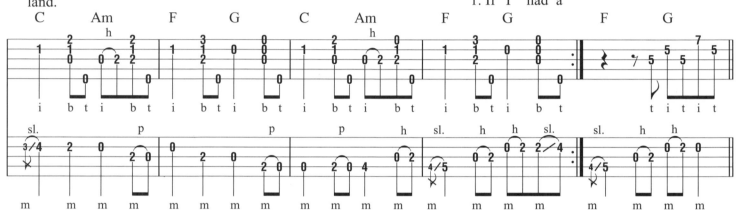

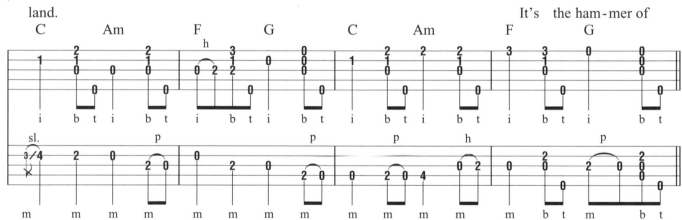

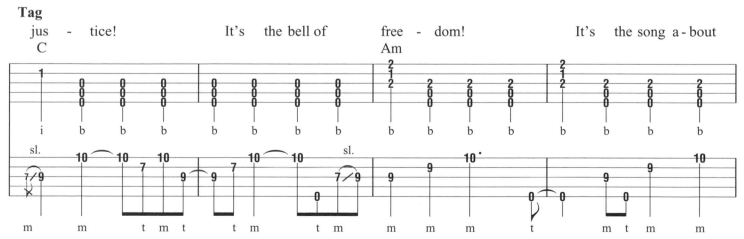

29

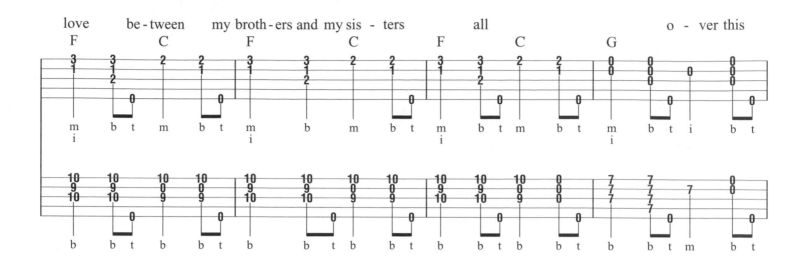

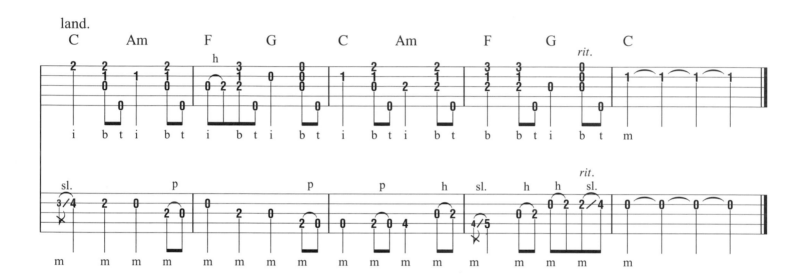

Additional Lyrics

2. If I had a bell,
I'd ring it in the morning.
I'd ring it in the evening
All over this land.
I'd ring out danger,
I'd ring out warning.
I'd ring out love between
My brothers and my sisters
All over this land.

3. If I had a song,
I'd sing it in the morning.
I'd sing it in the evening
All over this land.
I'd sing out danger,
I'd sing out warning.
I'd sing out love between
My brothers and my sisters
All over this land.

4. Well I got a hammer
And I got a bell
And I've got a song to sing
All over this land.
It's the hammer of justice,
It's the bell of freedom.
It's the song about love between
My brothers and my sisters
All over this land.

Kisses Sweeter than Wine

Words by Ronnie Gilbert, Lee Hays, Fred Hellerman and Pete Seeger
Music by Huddie Ledbetter

Key of G

G tuning:
(5th-1st) G-D-G-B-D

Intro

Moderately fast ♩ = 132

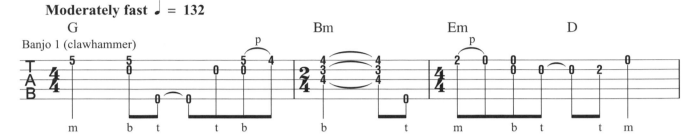

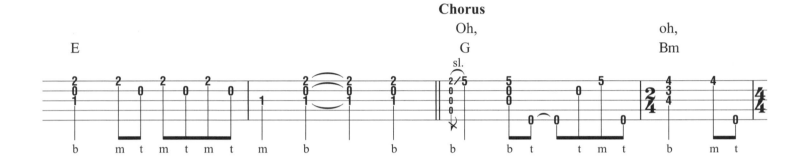

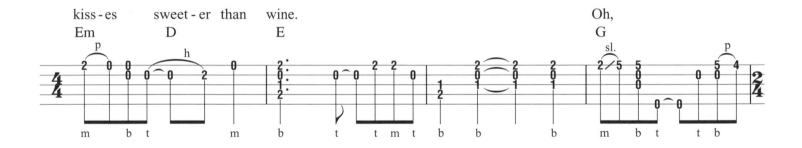

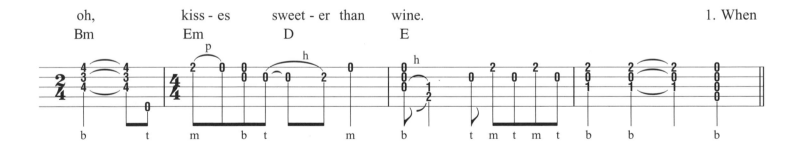

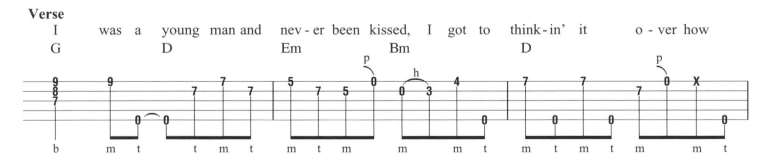

much I had missed. I got me a girl and I kissed her and then,

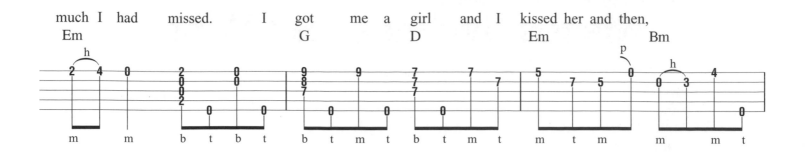

oh Lord, I kissed her a - gain.

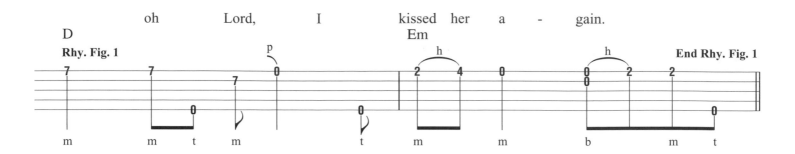

Chorus

Oh, oh, kiss-es sweet-er than wine.

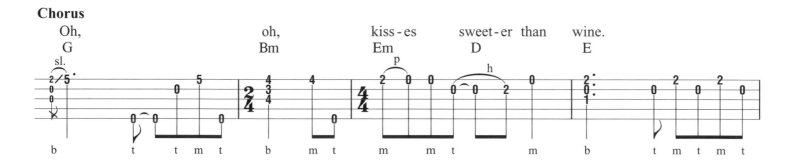

Oh, oh, kiss-es sweet-er than

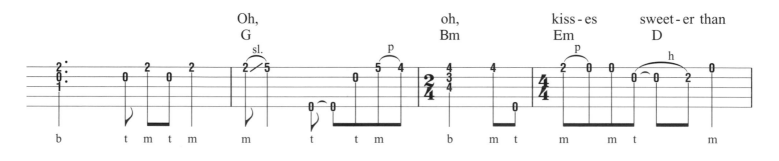

wine.

Verse

2. I asked her to mar-ry and
3. *See additional lyrics*

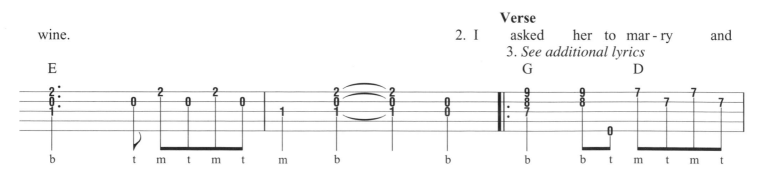

be my sweet wife. We'd be so hap-py the rest of our life. I

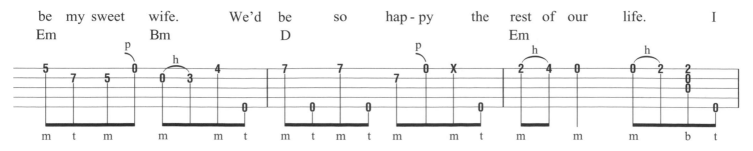

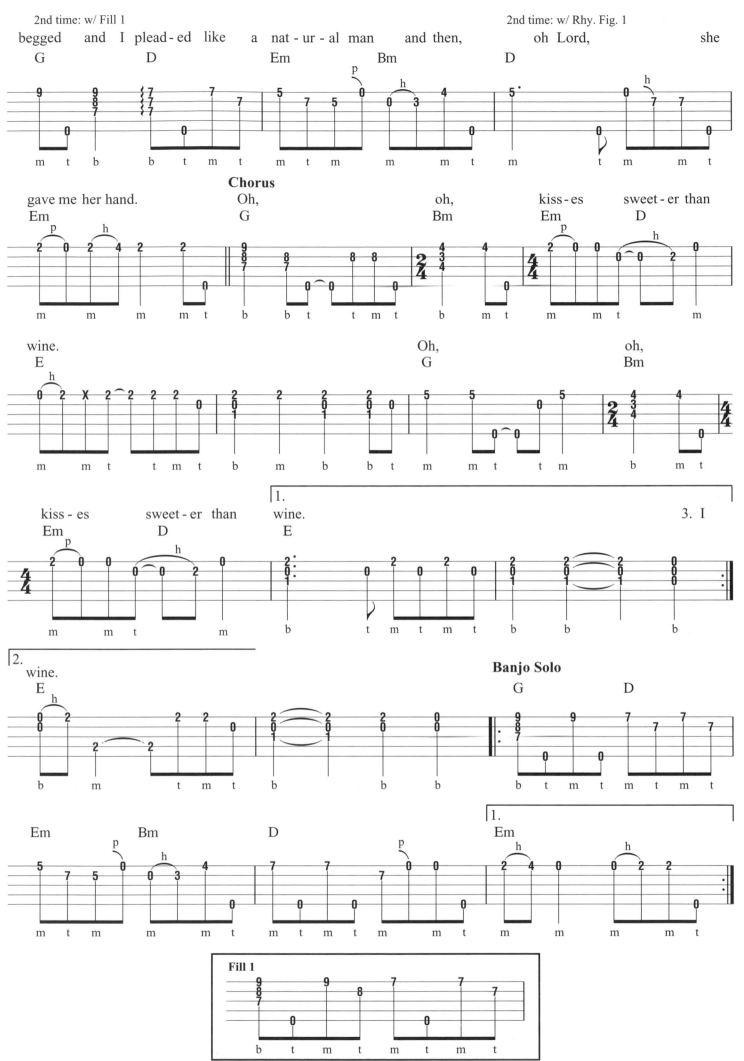

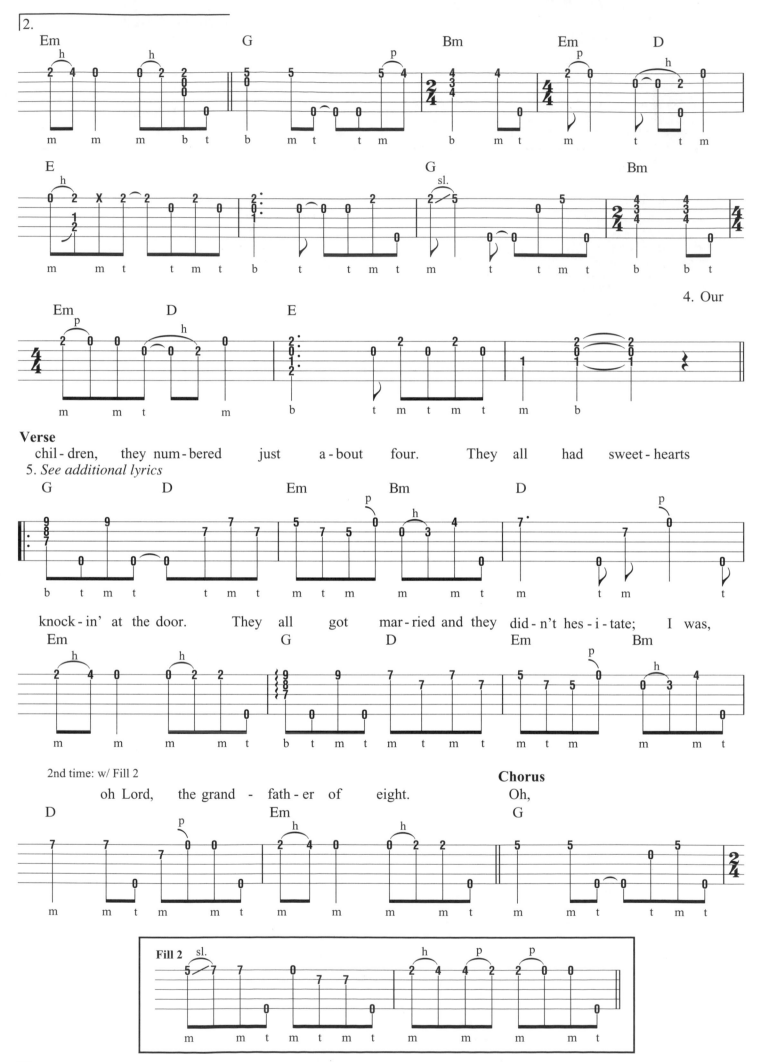

Verse

chil - dren, they num - bered just a - bout four. They all had sweet - hearts

5. *See additional lyrics*

knock - in' at the door. They all got mar - ried and they did - n't hes - i - tate; I was,

2nd time: w/ Fill 2

oh Lord, the grand - fath - er of eight.

Chorus

Oh,

oh,   kiss - es   sweet - er than   wine.

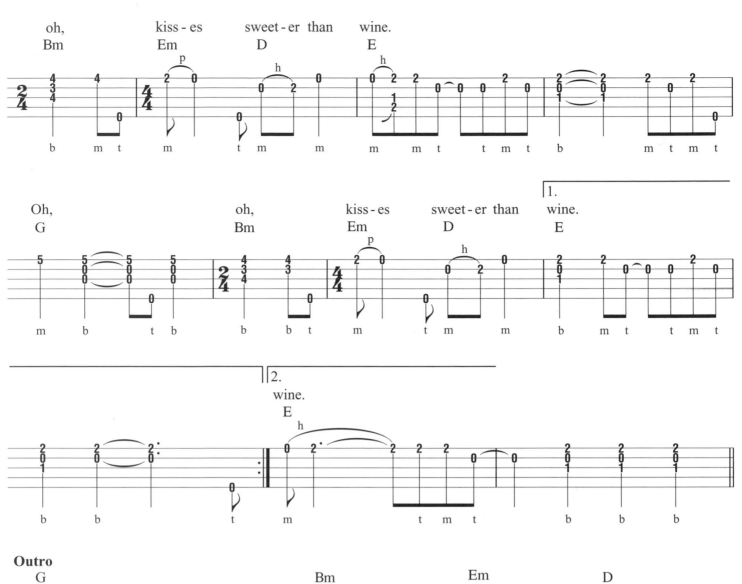

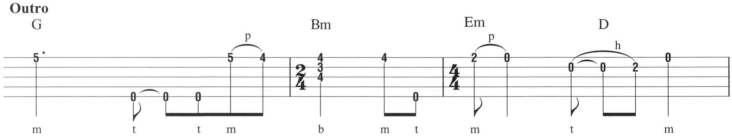

Outro

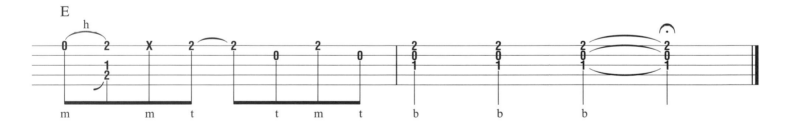

Additional Lyrics

3. I worked mighty hard and so did my wife,
   Workin' hand-in-hand to make a good life.
   With corn in the field and wheat in the bins
   And then, oh Lord, I was the father of twins.

5. Now that I'm old and ready to go,
   I get to thinking what happened a long time ago.
   Had a lot of kids, trouble and pain,
   But, oh Lord, I'd do it again.

Mbube
(Wimoweh)

Words and Music by Solomon Linda
Additional Words and Music by Ronnie Gilbert, Lee Hays, Fred Hellerman and Pete Seeger

Key of D

Banjo 1: C tuning, capo II:
(5th-1st) G-C-G-B-D

Banjos 2, 3, & 4: Double C tuning, capo II:
(5th-1st) G-C-G-C-D

Intro
Moderately fast

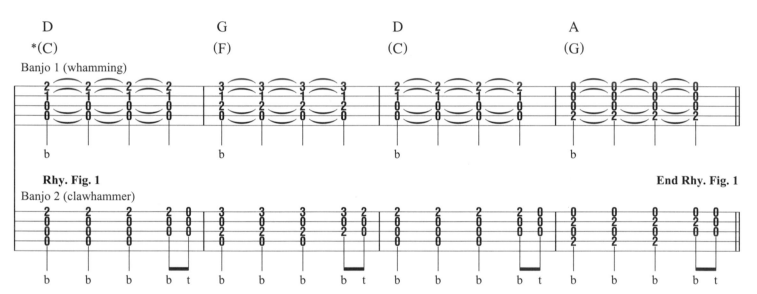

*Symbols in parentheses represent chord names respective to capoed banjos.
 Symbols above reflect actual sounding chords. Capoed fret is "0" in tab.

Verse

Banjo 2: w/ Rhy. Fig. 1 (13 times)

Weh, uh,   ha,   wim - o - weh,

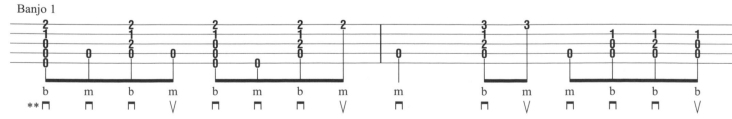

**□ = downstroke, V = upstroke

wim - o - weh,   wim - o - weh.

D   A

(C)   (G)

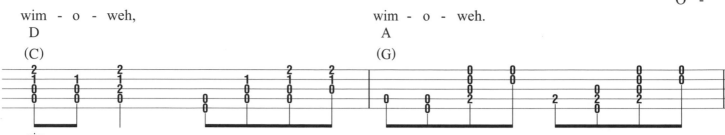

sim.

wim - o - weh, o - wim - o - weh, o - wim - o - weh, o - wim - o - weh, o -
Weh, uh,   ha,   wim - o - weh,

D   G

(C)   (F)

wim - o - weh, o - wim - o - weh, o - wim - o - weh, o - wim - o - weh. O -
wim - o - weh,   wim - o - weh.

D   A

(C)   (G)

wim - o - weh, o - wim - o - weh, o - wim - o - weh, o - wim - o - weh, o -
Weh, uh,   ha,   wim - o - weh,

D   G

(C)   (F)

Uh,

wim - o - weh, o - wim - o - weh, o - wim - o - weh, o - wim - o - weh. O -
wim - o - weh,   wim - o - weh.

D   A

(C)   (G)

whoa,   oh,   uh,   whoa,   oh,   uh,

wim - o - weh, o - wim - o - weh, o - wim - o - weh, o - wim - o - weh, o -

Weh, uh,   ha,   wim - o - weh,

D   G

(C)   (F)

Rhy. Fig. 2

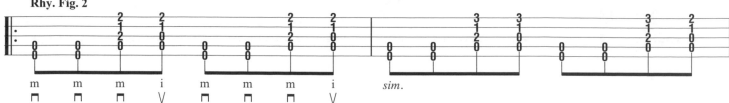

whoa,   oh,   oh,   oh.   Uh,

wim - o - weh, o - wim - o - weh, o - wim - o - weh, o - wim - o - weh. O -

wim - o - weh,   wim - o - weh.

D   A

(C)   (G)

End Rhy. Fig. 2

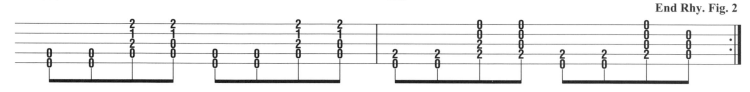

We,   de,   de,   de,

whoa,   oh,   uh,   whoa,   oh,   uh,

wim - o - weh, o - wim - o - weh, o - wim - o - weh, o - wim - o - weh, o -

Weh, uh,   ha,   wim - o - weh,

D   G

(C)   (F)

we,   oh,   bum,   bu,   weh.

whoa,   oh,   oh,   oh.   Uh,

wim - o - weh, o - wim - o - weh, o - wim - o - weh, o - wim - o - weh. O -

wim - o - weh,   wim - o - weh.

D   A

(C)   (G)

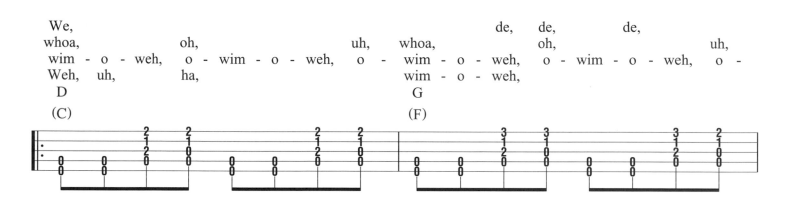

Banjo 1: w/ Rhy. Fig. 2 (6 times)

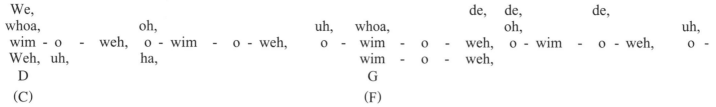

* **Rhy. Fig. 3**
Banjo 3 (clawhammer)

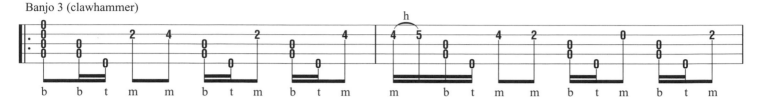

*Played with even eighth notes.

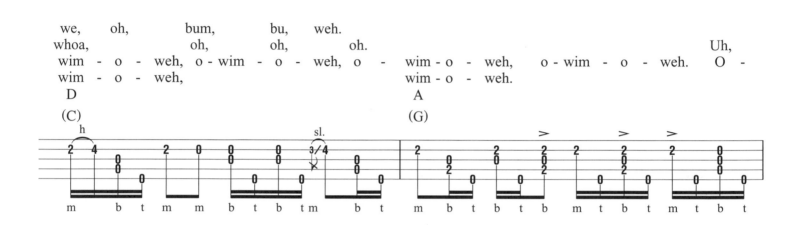

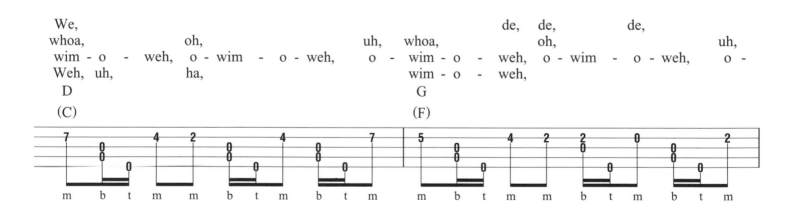

End Rhy. Fig. 3

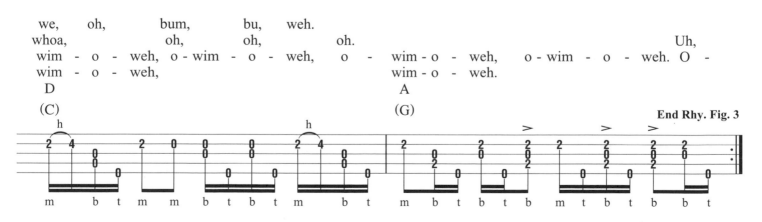

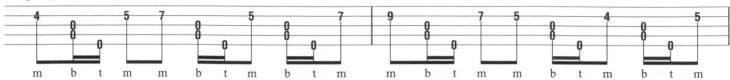
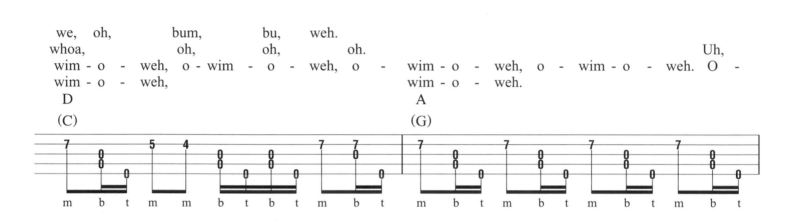
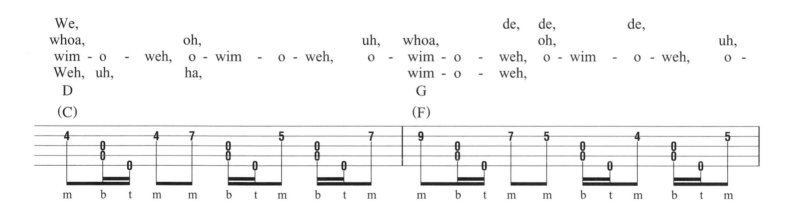
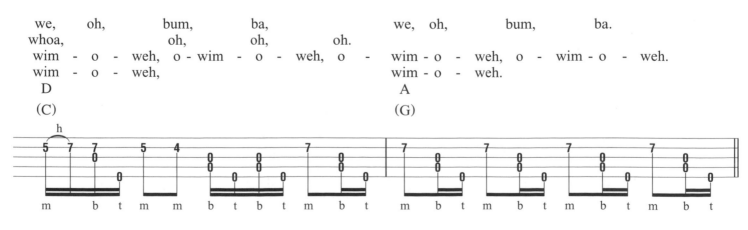

Outro

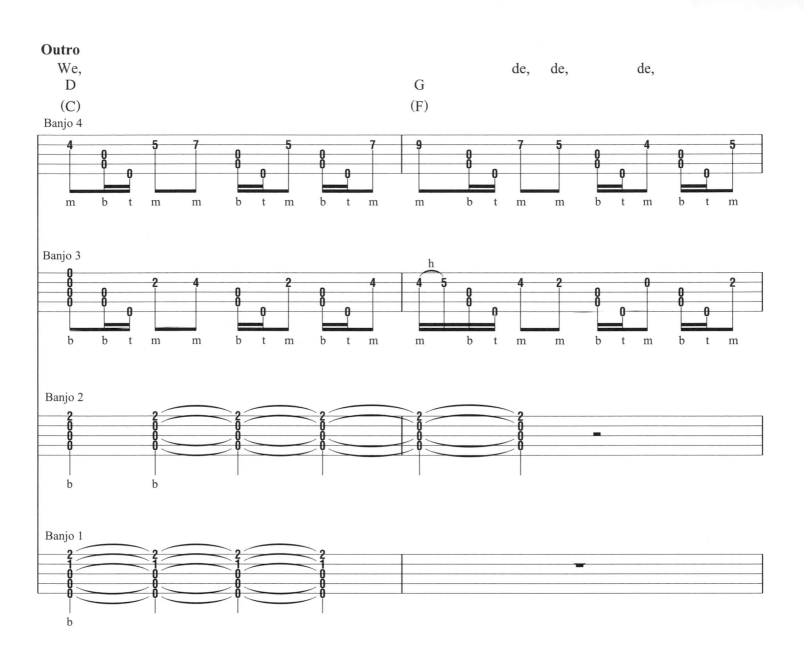

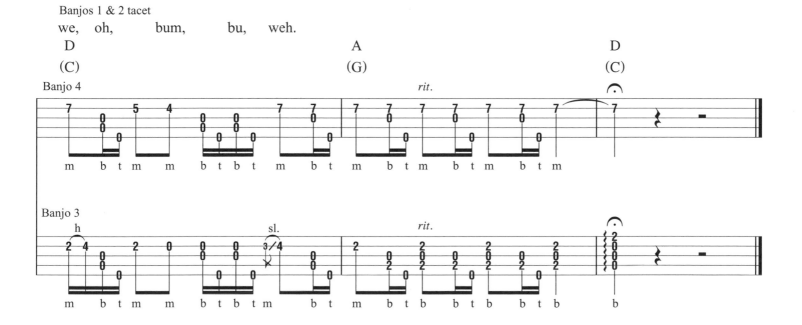

Turn! Turn! Turn!
(To Everything There Is a Season)

Words from the Book of Ecclesiastes
Adaptation and Music by Pete Seeger

Key of A

G tuning, capo II:
(5th-1st) G-D-G-B-D

Intro
Moderately fast ♩ = 148

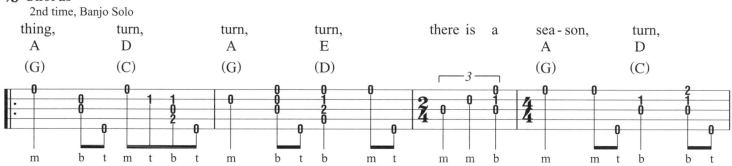

*Symbols in parentheses represent chord names respective to capoed banjo.
Symbols above reflect actual sounding chords. Capoed fret is "0" in tab.

 Chorus

2nd time, Banjo Solo

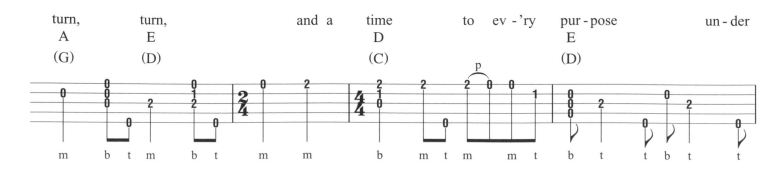

2nd time, Banjo Solo

heav-en.   1. A time to be born, a time to die, a time to
            4. *See additional lyrics*

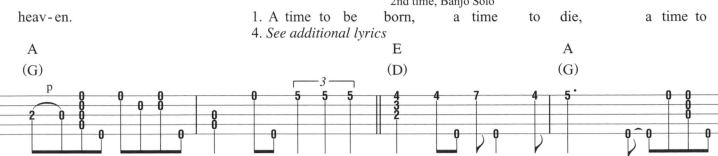

plant,   a time   to   reap,   a time   to   kill,   a time   to   heal,   a time   to

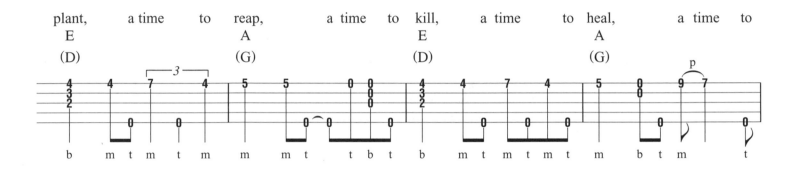

To Coda ⊕

laugh,   a   time   to   weep.   To ev-'ry-

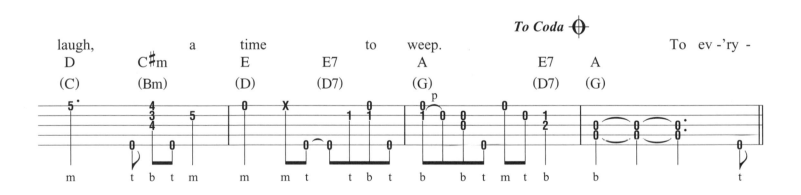

Chorus

thing,   turn,   turn,   turn,   there is a   sea-son,   turn,

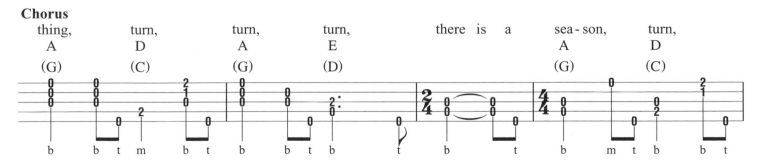

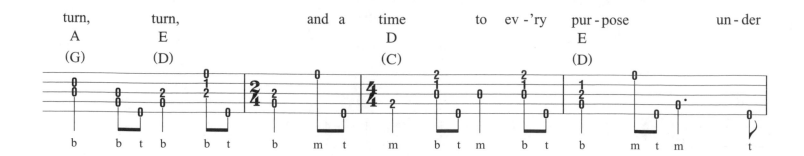

turn, turn, and a time to ev -'ry pur - pose un - der

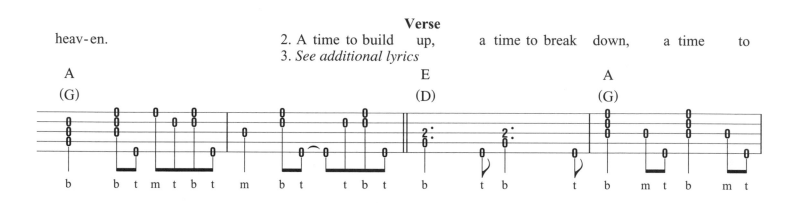

heav-en.

Verse

2. A time to build up, a time to break down, a time to

3. *See additional lyrics*

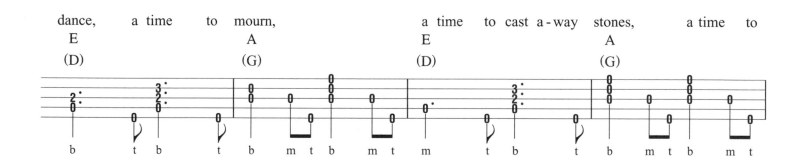

dance, a time to mourn, a time to cast a - way stones, a time to

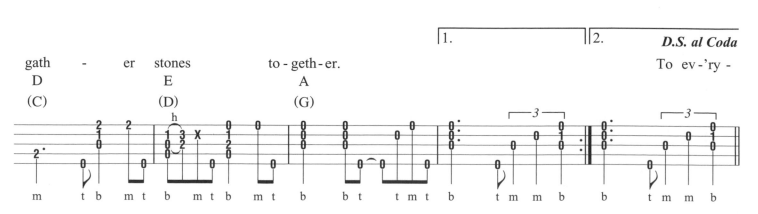

gath - er stones to - geth - er. To ev -'ry -

1.

2.

D.S. al Coda

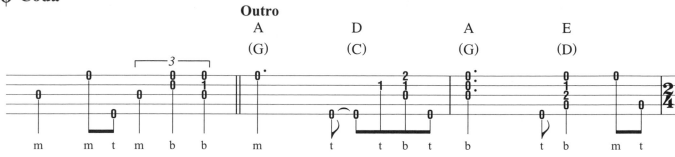

Outro

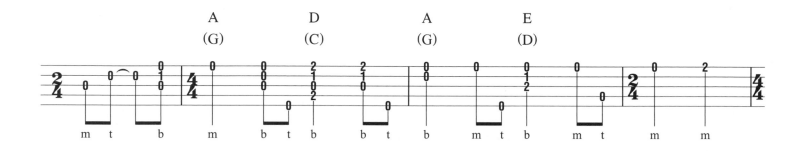

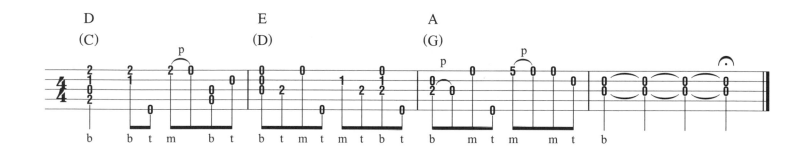

Additional Lyrics

3. A time of love, a time of hate,
   A time of war, a time of peace,
   A time you may embrace,
   A time to refrain from embracing.

4. A time to gain, a time to lose,
   A time to rend, a time to sew,
   A time for love, a time for hate,
   A time for peace, I swear it's not too late.

Sailing Down My Golden River

Words and Music by Pete Seeger

Key of D

Double C tuning, capo II:
(5th-1st) G-C-G-C-D

Intro

Moderately, in Two ♩ = 112

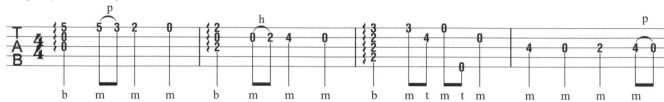

Banjo 1 (clawhammer)

*Symbols in parentheses represent chord names respective to capoed banjo.
Symbols above reflect actual sounding chords. Capoed fret is "0" in tab.

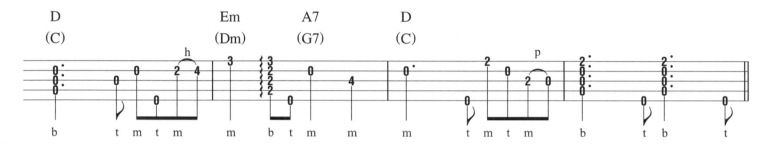

𝄋 Verse

1. Sail-ing down my   gold - en   riv - er,   sun   and wa-ter   all   my   own,⟩
3. Sail-ing down this   wind - ing high-way,   trav - el - ers   from   near   and   far,⟩

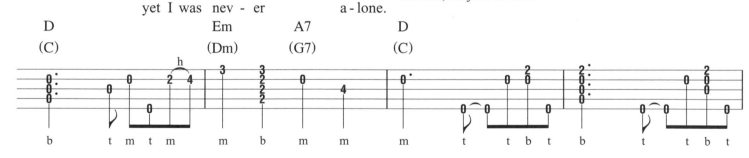

yet I was nev - er   a - lone.

2nd time, Banjo 1: w/ Fill 1

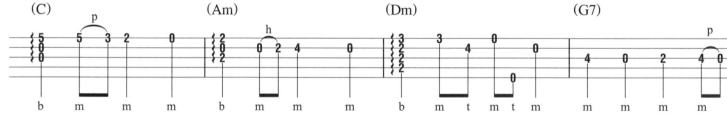

Fill 1

Banjo 1

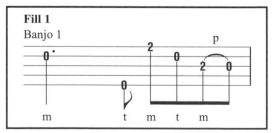

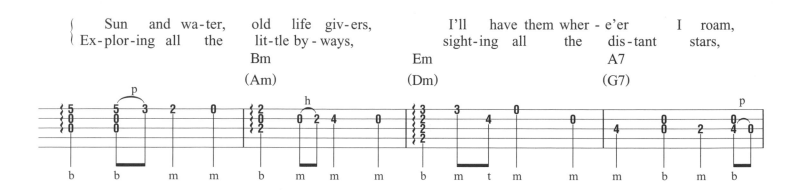

Sun and wa-ter, old life giv-ers, I'll have them wher-e'er I roam,
Ex-plor-ing all the lit-tle by-ways, sight-ing all the dis-tant stars,

To Coda $\oplus$ **Interlude**

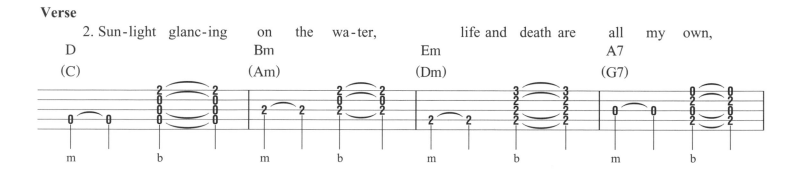

and I was not far from home.
yet I was not far from...

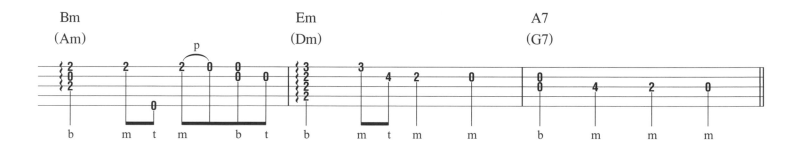

Verse

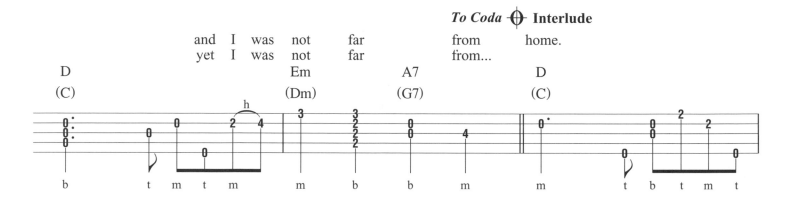

2. Sun-light glanc-ing on the wa-ter, life and death are all my own,

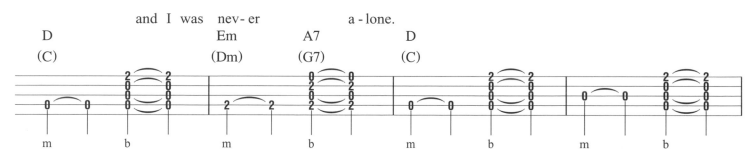

and I was nev-er a-lone.

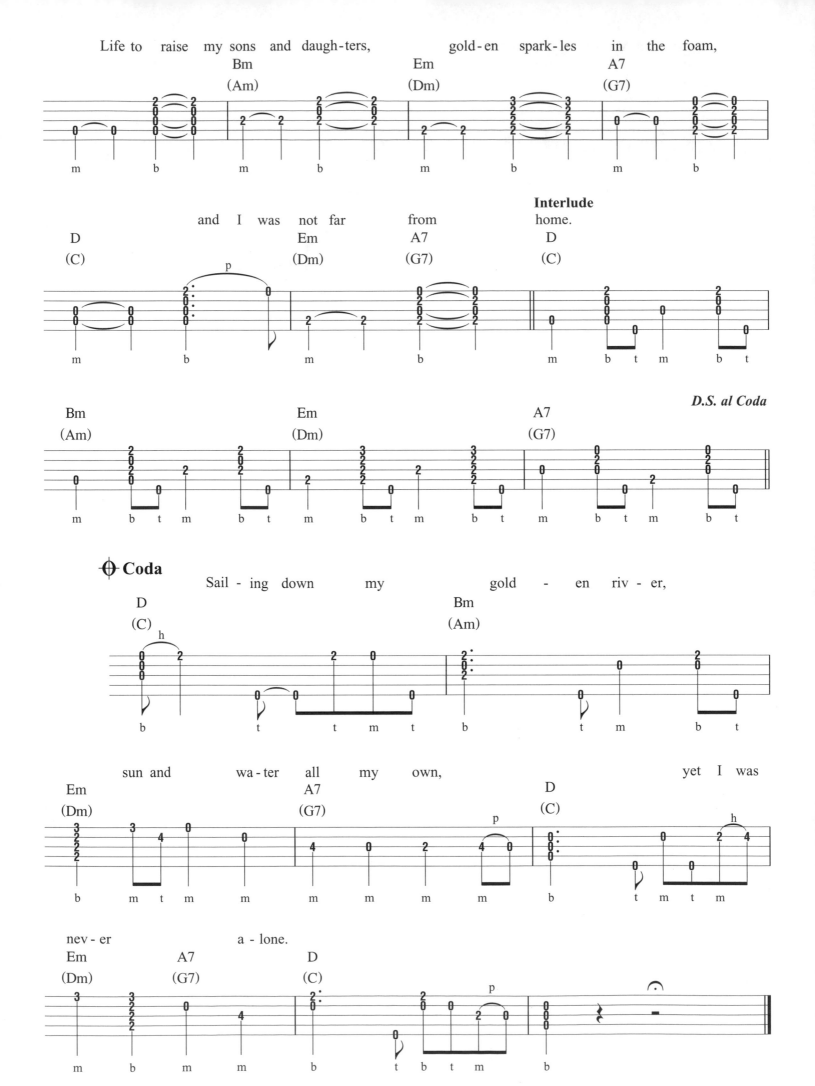